Jacob's Story

A JOURNEY OF FAITH

John Agliata

ACW Press
Phoenix, Arizona 85013

Jacob's Story: A Journey of Faith
Copyright ©2002 John Agliata
All rights reserved

Cover Design by
Interior design by Pine Hill Graphics

Packaged by ACW Press
5501 N. 7th Ave., #502
Phoenix, Arizona 85013
www.acwpress.com
The views expressed or implied in this work do not necessarily reflect those of
ACW Press. Ultimate design, content, and editorial accuracy of this work is the
responsibility of the author(s).

Library of Congress Cataloging-in-Publication Data

Agliata, John.
    Jacob's story : a journey of faith / by John Agliata.
 --1st ed.
    p. cm.
    ISBN 1-892525-73-9

    1. Consolation. 2. Infants (Newborn)--Death--
Religious aspects--Christianity. 3. Bereavement--
Religious aspects--Christianity. 4. Prayer--
Christianity. I. Title.

BV4907.A35 2002   248.8'66
                      QBI02-701264

All rights reserved. No part of this book may be reproduced, stored in a
retrieval system, or transmitted in any form or by any means–electronic,
mechanical, photocopying, recording, or otherwise–without prior permission in
writing from the copyright holder except as provided by USA copyright law.

Printed in the United States of America.

For "Uncle" Larry DeLozier
A true light on God's path

Chapter One

"Please, Lord, Save My Child"

"Have you been leaking any fluid?"

Six words. Six small words.

I looked at Carla, my wife of almost three-and-a-half years, lying on her back, her shirt lifted and pants scooched down. A big glob of ultrasound goop was spread across her once-flat belly that had recently begun to show a little pooch. Her eyes were scared, confused.

Suddenly, I shivered. What had been a hot summer afternoon seemed in an instant to turn frighteningly frigid, but it was a different kind of cold than I'd ever experienced before. It wasn't the type of cold that can be combated with a warm coat. This cold was on the inside and, oddly enough, I thought of the time I received intravenous antibiotics and the drugs flowed into my body colder than my blood. Now, instead of in just my forearm, it felt like that throughout my body.

Jacob's Story

"Have you been leaking any fluid?"

What kind of question was that?

"No," Carla responded, barely above a whisper. Her hand, which had been resting peacefully in mine as we anticipated seeing our child for the first time on a tiny monitor, suddenly squeezed hard around my fingers, hard enough to make me jump.

I looked at the ultrasound technician, staring intently at the monitor. Her eyes darted all around the small screen, searching.

"This isn't good," she said in a low voice. They sounded like words not meant for our ears, words that spilled out in the intensity of the moment from a woman who knew she was going to be the bearer of bad news to a hopeful young couple. Abruptly, she pushed the "stop" button on the VCR that was to have recorded the first pictures of our child, a video to be copied and sent to relatives near and far, the original locked away in a safe deposit box to protect it from fire, floods and burglars. "I'm going to get the doctor."

She left quickly, the breeze stirred by her passing filled with a light hint of flowery perfume. As the door closed slowly behind her, I put my head down, leaning forward on the table where Carla lay. My heart beat fast, much faster than the ticking of my watch, which now seemed loud and out of proportion.

I don't know how long we sat there. What seemed like hours probably was no more than ten minutes, but in those ten minutes things were said, things were done that would set the course we would travel for the next four months.

"This doesn't sound good," Carla said in a voice that time had taught me meant she was struggling to hold back tears. Looking up at her watery eyes, all I could do was shake my head, fighting back tears of my own. "What are we going to do?" she asked shakily.

It wasn't so much a question as a cry for help. Nothing made sense. We'd been blindsided by something we had talked about—hinted around, more accurately—but never actually

A Journey of Faith

imagined would come true, and Carla was reaching for something to hold on to.

"No matter what, honey, we will make it through this," I promised, surprised at the conviction in my voice knowing the fright and sadness welling up inside of me. "We will. I promise you I will be here for you no matter what, and we will get through this, I promise you."

Silently, I put my head back down. And I prayed. That prayer—laying myself bare before God and saying "You have me. I now know what it means to rely totally on You. Please, Lord, help"—was one I would repeat many times during the next four months. It was close in some ways to the prayers that had dominated my youth, but in another way, it was totally different. In my youth, the prayers had been to help me out of jams I had gotten myself in—not studying for a test and praying for snow that night, breaking a window with a baseball and praying my parents would somehow not notice. Now, my prayer was pure: "Please, Lord, save my child."

Chapter Two

"Trying"

That child, who would be named Jacob Alexander Agliata, was conceived on April 27, 2000, amid ceiling-high stacks of boxes and discarded empty rolls of packing tape. One minute we were packing, stuffing and sealing yet another box in preparation for our move from our basement apartment to our soon-to-be-completed home about 30 minutes away in Trenton, Ohio, and the next minute we were "trying."

That word "trying" had been a central part of our lives for several months. It was such an annoying word to me, a word that did all it could to take the intimacy out of the act of making love with the purpose of creating a child. It was a word, frankly, that I tried to put out of my mind while we were in the act of "trying."

Somehow, amidst the clutter of boxes, piles of to-be-donated items and stacked furniture, we did something that day that we had been unable to do the previous three months. We created a life.

We arrived at the decision to start "trying" fairly easily, which is typical for Carla and me. We have the tendency to make major life decisions fairly simply. Part of that is because time has shown us that in almost every case, our first choice is the right choice. Deciding to "try" came about in one 15-minute conversation. One weekend afternoon we were sitting on the couch in our dark, smelly basement apartment (hardly the atmosphere for romance) and the topic came up. It had come up before. In fact, on our honeymoon three years earlier, we spent time lounging on a beach in Hawaii with pen and paper in hand, thinking about the logistics of having a baby and had gone over all the questions.

"Can we afford to have this baby?" Well, no, but who can ever afford to have a baby? We'd make do, we'd sacrifice, and we'd raise our child well.

"Can we go without sleep?" Well, no. In fact, Carla had and still has a strong affinity for sleep. Whereas I can function on four to six hours, Carla could get ten and still feel the need for an afternoon nap.

"Are you ready to change diapers?" This question was for me, as Carla knew she was. She'd done it before. Really messy diapers too, from what I'd heard. I, however, had never come close to changing a diaper. But I would learn, for the good of my future child and the peace of my marriage.

The conversation that day in our basement apartment didn't directly deal with any of these questions. We both were of the opinion that if you thought too hard about whether you should have a baby, you would never actually take the plunge, so to speak, and the human race would eventually die. So in the end, while a hockey game unfolded on the television in front of us, it came down to:

"You wanna?"

"Sure."

"When?"

"No time better than the present."

"OK. Let's go."

"Can we leave the game on?"

Just kidding on that last one. Really.

The first month of "trying" was amazing. All of a sudden, sex had a higher purpose. And that seemed to make the actual act even more enjoyable than it was before. By the time the end of the month came around, we both just *knew* we were pregnant. Neither of us said a thing about it, though. I wrote about it in my journal. Carla kept it in her thoughts. It was the unspoken "it" in our marriage. We would sit at dinner and talk about our work days, and I'd go on and on about this situation or that meeting when the only real thing on my mind—the thing I wanted to blurt out more than anything else—was, "So did your period start?" Not exactly the most appropriate dinnertime conversation, but certainly no worse than some things my sister and I had said to each other across the dinner table when we were children.

Behind all of this was the arrogance—especially prevalent in males—that plagues many young couples who decide to try to get pregnant. After all, I was doing everything right. I was wearing boxers, not briefs. I had stopped riding my bicycle. I was avoiding warm baths. And, by God, I was male. How could we *not* be pregnant?

Easily, as it turned out. Carla came out of the bathroom one late afternoon with a frown on her face. She plopped down next to me on the couch and folded herself into my arms.

"It started," she said and buried her head in my chest.

A Journey of Faith

This was one of those moments that tests a husband's worth, one of those times when we can either prove our value to our spouses or solidify the misperception that we really aren't that essential in the grand scheme of things. As much as I wanted to try to cheer her up, to say, "Hey, we might not be pregnant yet, but now we get another month of trying! And this month was fun, wasn't it?" it was much better for me to simply say, "I'm sorry. We'll get there," and kiss her forehead.

Chapter Three

Finding God in Charleston

"We'll get there." Those three words describe many things in my life with Carla, including our religious journeys. I'm a huge advocate now of couples waiting until they are of the same religious persuasion before getting serious. Of course, I didn't follow my own advice way back when. In fact, when Carla and I met as freshmen at Drake University in Des Moines, Iowa, we were at opposite ends of the religious spectrum.

Carla was a tried-and-true Lutheran, as her father was before her and his father before him. There really was never a question whether Carla would grow up Lutheran. It was just the way things were. Sunday mornings were spent in the pews of Immanuel Lutheran Church in Wentzville, Missouri, where she and her two sisters wrote notes back and forth to each other in between listening to the sermon, standing when they

A Journey of Faith

were supposed to stand and sitting when they were supposed to sit. By the time I met Carla, she was a world ahead of me when it came to God. Simply put, she knew Him, though not in a personal way. The drawback of her unquestioned upbringing was that her religion really wasn't hers. She believed things because that's what she'd been taught to believe, not because they necessarily made any sense to her. It was an impersonal religion, blessed with assurances of who God was but lacking in any real relationship with Him. Nonetheless, she had a strong base on which to build.

I, on the other hand, had been raised without any religious foundation. My father, a non-practicing Catholic, and my mother, a sometimes-practicing Episcopalian, made that decision before my sister and I were born, and it's a decision they both say they would probably make differently if they had it to do over again. I had the basic concept of what God was all about, but I had no idea what the Bible actually said, what God's promises were and what different people believed and why. My childhood wasn't filled with anything that motivated me to seek Him. And without a true foundation, I stumbled around during my younger teen years trying to make sense of feelings I had that there was something more, not just for me but for everyone.

In retrospect, I realize I was blessed by the fact that God always seemed to bring people with strong religious foundations in my life. When the first question of "What's it all about?" hit, it was a friend named Holly, who was open to debating religious issues with me for hours on the phone. While most teens gossiped about who was dating whom, Holly and I talked about how to become a Christian, conflicts between Christianity and the science we were learning in school and the importance of a relationship with the Creator. When I got to college, more than 1,000 miles away from my suburban New York home, Holly handed me off to Carla who became God's witness in my life.

Jacob's Story

Still, I can't honestly say our dating life centered on God. It was more of the typical college romance, centered on hormones, cheap dates and too much freedom. In fact, most of the time when we did talk about God, it was more of an assault by me on Carla's "traditional" beliefs. How could she blindly accept something without questioning it? How could she believe in the Bible with all its contradictions? Why didn't she use her own mind to figure out her own beliefs? Carla, to her credit, took my assault in stride and stayed strong in her faith. In the process, she planted the seeds of sensible Christianity in my heart. She also began to examine her own beliefs and, through prayer, wrestled with some of the inconsistencies between what she was told to believe and what she felt God was telling her was true through His Word. That introspection led her to move away from the Lutheran church to a belief in and relationship with God that was more her own and formed by how she saw God working in the world. As the saying goes, it was more relationship and less religion.

I, of course, took this move as a great victory for my battle against organized religion. After all, who needed a church congregation? My relationship with God was my business and I didn't need to share it with anyone in any sort of church service, regardless of what the Bible said about fellowship. There was one slight problem with this, however. It wasn't God's plan.

As Carla moved slightly away from her roots in Lutheranism, I was blindsided during the holiday season of 1995 to start going to church. There's really no other way to explain it. One day I was vehemently against organized religion, the next day I felt this strong tug to start attending, to shut my mouth and to learn. I can even remember the specific moment. Carla and I had gone to visit my parents over the Christmas holidays of our last college year. We had become engaged a few months before and were starting to plan for our wedding. We were driving back from a New Year's Eve dinner in downtown Charleston, South Carolina, and, all of a sudden,

A Journey of Faith

it was in my heart: Go to church. Learn about Me. Here's My hand. Take it.

In the subsequent four years, Carla and I grew in Christ together. I dove into the Bible and, for about a year straight, just read. When I was tempted to ask defying questions, I shut my mouth and prayed. Without fail, God answered my prayers and, most of the time, what was confusing soon made sense. When Carla and I got married in March 1997, I took on the biblical role of spiritual leader. All of a sudden, the guy who was so vehemently against organized religion was helping the life-long Christian delve into the intricacies of God's Word. Through our relationship with God, our relationship with each other grew to a new level.

Carla and I discussed a range of religious issues, from the most basic to those that stump the most intelligent religious scholar. Where I was weak, Carla strengthened me. Where Carla was weak, I strengthened her. It was the closest I had ever come to actually seeing God's hand at work in our lives and I learned a simple but glorious truth: God can do amazing things. He can take two people on opposite ends of the religious spectrum and bring them together in His loving arms.

It wasn't always easy. Our struggles to find the right church were many, as were our conflicts over how we should live our lives now that we knew what we believed God was about. But through it all, we felt God with us, telling us, "Don't worry. We'll get there."

Chapter Four

Getting There

It was a late May afternoon when we found out "we got there" on another front. I had come home an hour early from my job as publisher of *The Oxford Press*, a local weekly newspaper, hoping to take advantage of the increased daylight to play some tennis with Carla. Actually, I should say, play something that resembled tennis, because the game Andre Agassi, Pete Sampras and the Williams sisters play would appear to the observer as vastly different from the game Carla and I played.

I sat down at the computer, unwinding a bit, while Carla tinkered about our uprooted apartment, now in the final stages of preparation before our move. Then she reached over my shoulder and handed me a small, wrapped present. I wasn't surprised. It was not unlike Carla to pick me up a little something while she was out shopping. As I tore open the wrapping paper, my first thought was that she had bought me a barbeque meat thermometer.

"How odd," I thought. "I already have a meat thermometer that works quite well, and she knows that too." I had just barbequed the night before. But maybe she'd forgotten. Maybe she just wanted to make sure I *really* knew when our dinner was ready. Or maybe she just thought I needed a new and better meat thermometer. Whatever the case, it was a touching gesture.

And then, as I tore away the last of the wrapping paper, I saw the marking on the "meat thermometer," two parallel lines less than an inch in length. Above that, I saw some printing that read, "One line, not pregnant. Two lines, pregnant." My jaw hit the floor. I turned in my seat and looked up at Carla, who by this time was trying unsuccessfully to stop the tears of joy from flowing down her face.

"You're going to be a daddy," she said, choked up with the same emotion that instantly flooded over me. I jumped up and hugged her, laughing and crying at the same time. A daddy! Me! As I hugged Carla, I realized that in between us now was a tiny, living, growing part of us. And, as any overprotective father-to-be would do, I hugged her a little less tightly, not wanting to hurt the baby.

When I announced our pending arrival to the readers of my weekly *Oxford Press* newspaper column I wrote that Carla's words—You're going to be a daddy—"are the most life-changing six words I can imagine." Ironic, I think now, about how six other words an ultrasound technician would utter would change my life so much more.

Pregnancy was blissful. In fact, things were going so well and so easily that I sometimes had to verbally remind myself that this was all reality. Carla's early pregnancy symptoms amounted to some morning queasiness, an insatiable appetite and a craving for cheddar cheese, corn dogs and burritos. At night, I would lay with my head on her belly, still flat and tight, and talk to our child, saying, "You better remind your mommy when you're a teen-ager and she gets mad at you how easy you are being on her now."

Thanks to a convenient bit of scheduling, we were able to tell our parents in person about their coming grandchild. My father was particularly keen on the idea of being a grandpa. When it got too troublesome to keep saying "he or she" or "him or her," he found a way around it. During a Fourth of July visit, he suggested finding a nickname to make it easier. Just then, a Kix cereal commercial came on the television.

"A nickname. Like Kix," he said.

Kix it was. And the timing seemed perfect for Kix's creation. My sister, Christy, two years my senior, was about a month further along in her first pregnancy than Carla, and the coming of our children formed a bond between the two of them that made me happy. Carla was the sister Christy never had…and probably often wished that I had been. They talked excitedly about how our children, so close in age, would grow up to be friends. My parents, now with two grandchildren on the way, were on top of the world.

We started preparing for our baby quickly and excitedly. The room in our house that I had insisted be called "the second guest room" during construction now switched to "the baby's room," and it began to take on the appearance of one. People asked us "Don't you worry that this will jinx things?" to which we would respond that this baby was either going to be fine and healthy or not fine, based on God's will, not some silly superstition.

While Carla began to go through the physical changes that accompany carrying a baby, I decided to show my commitment to the cause in a variety of ways. The first was the "Seven Steps to Poop-dom." People laughed when I told them that I was expecting a child but had never changed a diaper in my life.

A Journey of Faith

They found it funny, I guess, that a dad-to-be could be such a complete ignoramus when it came to one of the basic functions of a new parent. To show that I wasn't going to remain ignorant, I took a Saturday afternoon and drew up the Seven Steps to get me ready to change a poopy diaper. Carla was obviously all for the idea. Less than 24 hours after the drafting of the Seven Steps, I found myself seated on the couch, a Betsey Wetsey doll on my lap and a Huggies diaper in my hands.

The first thing that struck me was how incredibly tiny this diaper was, that it would actually fit our newborn baby. The second thing that struck me was how incredibly large this diaper was going to be on Betsey Wetsey. Not feeling confident enough to point this fact out to my diaper-experienced wife, I went ahead with the project, tucking the diaper under Betsey Wetsey's bottom and getting ready to Velcro it together. But when I folded it up over Betsey Wetsey's tummy, I realized that this diaper was going to cover much more than her bottom. It was going to be, in effect, a tiny baby straightjacket.

At this point, even I, a diaper dolt, had to stop in protest of the mockery this was making of the Seven Steps.

"This is so unrealistic!" I said, thinking I was free from Carla's diaper insanity.

Carla, however, was not to be denied. Quicker than I ever thought a pregnant woman could or would move, she bounded—yes bounded—up the stairs and came back with a stuffed bear I bought her back in college when we were dating.

"Here," she said. "Try this. It's a little more realistic."

Now, I know pregnancy can do weird things to a woman, but there's something a bit funny about your wife telling you that a stuffed bear is "a little more realistic" in relation to a baby. I didn't laugh, at least not outwardly, and I put the diaper on the bear, proving to Carla that I was indeed serious about being a full-service daddy.

On top of my diaper training, I also began to paint. Now, that is a harmless enough phrase for your average Joe. But

19

Jacob's Story

when it comes to painting, I'm not your average Joe. Give me a computer keyboard and an idea and I can turn a phrase, but put a loaded paintbrush in my hands and I have the reputation of being the Picasso version of Rambo: No one quite knows where the paint is going to go. It was a reputation I admit I earned during the summer before my last year in junior high. On a hot August morning, my mother left me with a bucket of blue paint, a few brushes and rollers and instructions to paint the stairwell leading down to the basement. What she returned to was a nightmare that looked as if the entire Smurf village had been hit by artillery. In the absence of clear instructions as to what exactly was meant by "paint the basement stairwell," I painted everything. And I mean everything. Did she want me to paint the handrail? Probably, I thought, so I painted it. What about the ceiling? I'm sure, I thought, so I painted that, too. I still hear about the blue specks of paint that somehow got on a silver-colored spaghetti pot.

With this nightmare lingering in the back of my mind like a war flashback, I picked up a paintbrush again and began to paint a Noah's Ark paint-by-number mural on the nursery wall. As I wrote in my weekly "My Mind" newspaper column, "It was with great trepidation that I picked up a brush again to begin work on something infinitely more important than a basement stairwell. I mean, my child will come home from the hospital and we will put him or her in a crib and he or she will be able to look at this mural that Daddy worked so hard on. It's easy enough to traumatize a child without making him or her look at a poorly painted mural.... But simply being in that room and anticipating all that is to come is motivation enough to help me keep it between the lines."

Chapter Five

"Have You Been Leaking Any Fluid?"

The ultrasound appointment was scheduled for 12:20 p.m. Wednesday, August 30. As the day neared, it became the only thing I could think about. We were going to get to see our child! I had written in my appointment book for that day "bring tape," and Carla had gone out and specifically bought the highest quality VCR tape she could find to record this occasion.

I went to work early that morning to accelerate the process of getting that week's newspaper to the presses. The air was already heavy with humidity as I stepped from my car into the office's small parking lot just before 8 a.m. I was happy. This was the day we would find out if it would be Rebekah Rose or Jacob Alexander.

We'd debated the pros and cons of finding out the baby's sex and ultimately decided that, since there's so much "new" in

Jacob's Story

a first pregnancy, we would have the ultrasound technician tell us if she saw anything that would give us a clue. In the days leading up to the appointment, we even conducted an e-mail "guess the sex" poll among our friends and family. While "boy" was an early favorite, "girl" came from behind like George W. Bush on election night and, as the appointment time drew near, had taken the lead. Not believing in jinxes, hexes or other superstitions, we had told everyone we knew about this appointment, and many were waiting anxiously by their computers for the verdict. I swung by home, changed my clothes from my stuffy business attire to more comfortable shorts and T-shirt, and Carla and I made our way to the appointment 30 minutes away, videotape in hand.

When we walked into the waiting room of the second-floor office, we knew we would be living the "waiting" part. The room was jammed with pregnant women and their spouses, parents, children, friends and assorted others. Carla checked in and was told the ultrasound technician was running behind so we should be prepared to get comfortable. That was fine with us. We were happy. We joked about the "healthy living" video that played in the waiting room, and I used my clairvoyant powers to accurately guess the answers to the questions I'd seen in each of our previous visits. There's something about being a daddy-to-be in an OB-GYN waiting room. I was proud, proud of how beautiful Carla looked and of how we had created a life between us that we knew we were ready to bring up right. Our joking around masked the apprehension of seeing our child for the first time, wondering in the deepest recesses of our minds if everything would be OK, if the fact that Carla hadn't felt our baby move yet at 19 weeks—though my sister had felt hers move numerous weeks before—was really something to worry about or just something that differs from woman to woman.

About 45 minutes after we got there, we were ushered into the sub-waiting room, a place I never knew existed before

A Journey of Faith

becoming a part of my wife's OB-GYN visits. Essentially, the sub-waiting room was a smaller, hotter version of the regular waiting room with fewer magazines and no healthy-living video. I compared it to the on deck circle in baseball. It was a great relief after 20 minutes that we welcomed the ultrasound technician, who led us into the room where we'd see our child for the first time.

I handed her the videotape, which she popped into the machine while Carla got on the table, pushed her pants down and lifted her shirt up, exposing her belly that was showing the first outward signs of pregnancy. I sat down beside her, holding her hand, as my heart accelerated in anticipation. Without too many words, the technician squirted the cold goop onto Carla's belly, took the receiver and searched for our child. I focused in on the screen but couldn't make anything out, which didn't worry me. Friends and family had told me ultrasound pictures are often recognizable only to delirious parents, who can somehow see everything on their baby, including his little toe.

"I can't make anything out," the technician said, barely above a whisper. Still, I was not alarmed. My mind translated her statement into something that meant the ultrasound equipment had failed. We'd be doing some more waiting, I figured, as she went and got another machine. At the worst we'd have to come back another day after the machine was fixed. It was then that she said the six words that truly were the most life-changing I could possibly imagine:

"Have you been leaking any fluid?"

The technician left and we were alone. The wait seemed to go on forever. Tears had formed, fallen and dried up, only to be replaced by more. I found myself shaking uncontrollably, and Carla calmly stroked my arm to help me gather my composure. Millions of thoughts raced through my mind.

How could this be? Did I do something wrong? Every sin I had committed in my life flashed before me, and I was suddenly sure this was punishment for living a life that falls short of what God wanted from me. What would Carla say when she found out this was all my fault? What would she do when she realized that because of me something was terribly wrong with our child? The mind is our worst enemy when we're panicked, and I was panicked.

"This doesn't sound good," Carla said, breaking the silence. I looked up at her. "What are we going to do?"

I pushed the thoughts of blame aside. Looking back now, I realize the God was in that room with us that day and that as soon as I opened my mind to His ways, He filled me with reality. It wasn't my fault. Yes, I had sinned in my life. We all have and we all do. None of us meet God's wishes for us. Yet He loves us the same. My mind raced through the Bible, almost tangibly turning page after page like a speed-reader. The oft-mistaken picture of God is that he is only about love and happiness and joy. But he is also a God that, the Bible shows, has a breaking point and does punish people severely. Noah's neighbors could testify to that. But nowhere, save for Jesus Christ, was an innocent punished for the sins of another. If God had issue with my sins enough to level punishment, He would be punishing me directly. Thus, I felt God assuring me, it wasn't about punishment; it was about something so much more. In that room, we were beginning to see God's plan for us and our child.

"No matter what, honey, we will make it through this," I promised, the words filled with a conviction that came from God's endless reserve of strength. "I will be here for you no matter what and we will get through this. I promise you."

I put my head back down and prayed. It was an odd feeling. Here I was, in the midst of a waking nightmare, yet I felt a hand on my shoulder, steadying me as this storm's first gale-force winds kicked up.

A Journey of Faith

When the door to the exam room opened, I slowly lifted my head and looked into the kind, calming eyes of Dr. Kim Bonar. Though Dr. Bonar had seen Carla before during regular OB-GYN appointments prior to our baby's conception, we hadn't settled on a regular doctor and had been seeing different ones in the seven-member group. Dr. Bonar just so happened to be the one at the office during the time of our ultrasound.

Some would say it was a coincidence. I don't believe in coincidences. Too many things would happen in the following four months that would make me see God's very real and guiding hand in our everyday lives, putting people in positions where we would intersect with them, some for the duration, some for only a few hours. Dr. Bonar was the first of God's angels for us.

She shook my hand firmly and introduced herself. She had big, brown eyes and short spikey hair that was, in a strange sense, disarming and bridged the gap between patient and doctor. Her lips were full, curved into a nervous smile that told me she really understood the fear that now gripped us at the very core. Without delay, she took the seat the ultrasound technician had previously occupied. She had an air of confidence about her, of self-assuredness that let us know she was going to do whatever she could to help us. My mind danced quickly back to the prayer I had just prayed: "You have me. I now know what it means to rely totally on You. Please, Lord, help." Had God provided part of the answer so quickly?

More goop was put on Carla and the ultrasound receiver was again placed on her belly. Almost immediately, Dr. Bonar let out a relieved sigh.

"OK, there's the heartbeat," she said, pausing so Carla and I could look at the tiny beating force that sustained our child. I would learn later why Dr. Bonar's sigh had sounded so deep and relieved. The technician, unable to see anything, had written "fetal demise" on the chart that she had shown Dr. Bonar, so when she came into the office, she anticipated having to deliver the worst possible news.

25

Jacob's Story

Our momentary reprieve was short-lived, however. Dr. Bonar continued her scan of Carla and the baby. Even my untrained eye could make out a large black keyhole-shaped space in the middle of our child, a hole so big that it seemed to dwarf the rest of him. In a soft voice, Dr. Bonar gave us her initial assessment, the first in what would become a four-month crash course on fetal medicine.

There was no amniotic fluid around the baby. This fluid, which is a medical mystery even in this advanced age, cannot be replicated and its function cannot be duplicated. But the fluid hadn't leaked. Rather, it was what was causing that large, keyhole-shaped space, which was our baby's bladder. Amniotic fluid, we were told, is sucked in through the developing baby's mouth and excreted like urine. The process helps the baby's lungs learn how to work correctly. What had happened in our case, it appeared, was that a blockage was preventing the fluid from being excreted back into the uterus, where it would have provided the cushion that allows growing babies to have some padding in the womb and would have allowed the technician to see the baby more clearly.

The implications, we were told, could be far more serious than simply a blockage. Any amount of time a baby has in a low-fluid environment has a tendency to have an effect on lung development. And there was no telling what damage was being done to the kidneys and other internal structures by the backup of urine in the bladder. The problem Dr. Bonar had in making a diagnosis was that, like the ultrasound technician had said, she really couldn't see anything. We learned that ultrasounds are distinctive and readable because of the fluid around the baby, which provides contrast and allows observers to see the individual organs more clearly. With a sympathetic and reassuring smile, Dr. Bonar looked from Carla to me and back to Carla.

"The good news is that your baby has a heartbeat and if there's a heartbeat there's always hope," she said softly, almost motherly. "I won't lie to you. It doesn't look good. But we're going to find out exactly what it is and see if we can do anything to help." Our appointment ended with a load of uncertainty and a referral to a specialist in Cincinnati who could do a more powerful ultrasound.

The moments following Dr. Bonar's exit from the room were a blur. I got up and realized I felt nauseous so I sat back down. At some point, the ultrasound technician, who had stopped the VCR as soon as she had discovered a problem, placed the tape in my hand. She then ushered us to the billing and insurance office, where we numbly answered questions about our coverage as the two kind ladies attempted to set up appointments with specialists as quickly as possible. We needed two appointments, one with a perinatologist who would do a Level II ultrasound, and one with a geneticist, who would interview us about our chromosomal history.

"No, next week will not do," one of the woman in the office said emphatically into the phone. "We're talking emergency. We need something today or tomorrow."

More of God's angels doing their thing.

While the insurance people worked on getting us appointments, we were sent to another building in the sprawling hospital medical complex so Carla could have a blood test called a triple screen, which would indicate whether or not our baby's problem was chromosomal. Immediately we were confronted with how much things had changed in such a short amount of time. This new reality filled with the uncertainty of our baby's health was so harsh. We sat and answered the outpatient registration secretary's questions about our insurance and other information that seemed so inconsequential. When the secretary looked down at the blood test order, a routine order she'd probably processed hundreds of time for happy expectant mothers, she said, "Oh, you're pregnant! Congratulations!" We looked at

Jacob's Story

her with blank stares. What were we supposed to say? "Thank you" seemed out of the question. Going into the whole story was impossible. Forming a single word proved to be a challenge we couldn't meet. So we said nothing, and after an awkward, drawn-out pause, the secretary went on with her questions.

Shortly after, Carla was called back to have her blood drawn and I was alone in the waiting room. My head spun. What was happening here? This wasn't how things were supposed to go. People were waiting to hear if "Kix" was a boy or a girl, not whether he or she was going to live or not. I looked at my watch. My parents were waiting for an anniversary present from us. While they celebrated their thirtieth year as a married couple in a bed-and-breakfast in South Carolina, I later learned they were repeatedly checking their home answering machine for a message. The news I had to deliver was anything but what they expected.

With a quivering voice, I dialed their number on my cell phone. This was so messed up! I was supposed to be using this phone to deliver happy news. Instead, through tears, I left a message telling them that something was wrong with the baby, that there was no fluid around him, that we didn't know much more right now, but that they were trying to figure it out. I pushed "end" just as Carla returned, a Band-Aid attached to the underside of her left forearm.

I held her hand as we walked back to the insurance area. There was no good news for us there either. They hadn't been able to get us an appointment with the specialist we needed to see. They were going to keep trying, but the work day was nearing an end and they might not get through until tomorrow.

Tomorrow. It had never seemed further away. To think of waiting overnight without any knowledge of what the plan of action was seemed unbearable. This was all so out of control and I couldn't do anything to stop it.

"Why don't you guys just go home and we'll call you when we know something," the woman told us. She looked right into our eyes. "I promise you. We'll get you an appointment soon."

A Journey of Faith

We walked out of the medical complex numb. I held Carla's hand, my eyes fixed on the pavement. It had rained at some point while we were inside, and the air was heavy with the scents of late-summer flowers and recently cut grass. As we walked toward the car, I noticed a trash can out of the corner of my eye. Letting go of my wife's hand, I walked over, holding the videotape that was supposed to be a lifelong treasured keepsake of our first child above the open lid. How could I ever pop this video into the VCR and watch it? How could I ever put myself through that, remembering the day that our dreams for this child were pierced? I'm sure there were no more than 20 seconds of tape, but it was 20 seconds I did not want to ever see again. Opening my fingers, the tape landed at the bottom of the can with a thud.

Chapter Six

Darkest Hour, Brightest Hope

The house was as close to silent as a new, settling house can get when we got home. Even my excitable two-year-old dog, who normally greets us with barely controlled enthusiasm, seemed to recognize something was wrong and slinked up to Carla's leg with his ears pressed firmly back. We had left that home just a few hours before, laughing and joking, ready to see our child. What we came home to was vastly different.

This was our darkest hour. There's no other way to put it. Nothing that we had faced in our pasts, nothing that we would face in the coming four months and beyond, came close to the soul-wrenching sadness we felt that late afternoon. Despite my prayer in the doctor's office, my thoughts now were anywhere but on God. In His place was a set of entirely human emotions, unprepared to face something the magnitude of what we

A Journey of Faith

suddenly were facing. With my eye elsewhere, the door was opened to all sorts of harmful and negative things. Anger. Hate. Hopelessness.

For several hours I wandered around the house while Carla napped upstairs. Every time I sat down, I had the urge to move again. When the house couldn't contain a growing and increasingly troublesome rage that was building up inside me, I ventured outside and pulled any weed that had dared to grow in our lawn. All at once, just as it seemed as if that rage would come out, I was overcome by tears, followed by belly-deep sobs that I could not control. My God, what were we going to do? How could we possibly face this? What had we done wrong?

It took a good ten minutes before I was able to regain any semblance of composure and, with puffy, red eyes, I went back inside to find Carla on the couch. For a while, we didn't say anything. I stood there. She sat there. Then, finally, I spoke. When I did, it was as if the words were coming from far away, as if I were observing myself speaking instead of doing the actual speaking.

"I can't do this alone," I said. "I can't face this without help. We can't face this without help. We need prayers. I want to e-mail a prayer request to our friends."

Carla, pale and stone-faced, nodded.

Looking back at that moment, Carla notes how out of character it was for me to seek the help of others in a time of need. We'd known each other for eight years, been married for about three-and-a-half, and we'd gone through our share of ups and downs. The lowest of the lows was a bout of depression and anxiety attacks I suffered during our sophomore year in college. It was a time that saw me do my best to shut everyone out—friends, family, God and even her. If history was any indication, what Carla expected me to do when faced with something far worse than any depression or anxiety would be to get very quiet, avoid phone calls and e-mails, put on a happy face if someone asked if I was OK and keep everything bottled up inside.

31

Jacob's Story

God, however, had other plans. Asking Carla if I could send out a prayer request was the only thing that popped into my mind. It was the first thing I thought to do when I looked at the enormity of the situation we were facing. It was the only thing I felt I could do that was in my control. When I look at everything that happened because of that one decision to share our need with what was then a small group of friends, I realize that I will never again doubt the very real and very active hand of God in our everyday lives. There are those who hold the theory that if there is a God who created all that we see before us, He simply wound the clock that now runs freely, without His guiding hand, until it eventually stops. I don't have a rational, factual argument against that except to say this: I have lived something entirely different, something that has proven to me beyond a shadow of a doubt that God is active in our lives to further the glory of His kingdom on earth.

Silently, I went upstairs to our computer and typed a plea, my fingers moving unconsciously over the keyboard. God filled me with the words to reach out to ten people who would be the start of what would grow to be an enormous prayer chain. I wrote:

Subj: To our friends

Date: 8/30/00

This is probably the hardest thing I've ever had to write.

As most or all of you know, we went to get an ultrasound on the baby today. There are some serious problems. Basically, there is no fluid and without that fluid things don't look good. There is a heartbeat, but because there's no fluid, the scan can't pick up any of the anatomy (there's nothing to differentiate it). We are awaiting word for an appointment with a specialist to see if anything can be done and what exactly the diagnosis is.

I'm writing this to you because you are our friends. Please keep us in your prayers. We're not doing too good right now. I never thought we could hurt like this.

Love, John

I don't know exactly what I was expecting when I clicked "send." It was just something I felt compelled to do. Looking back, I realize part of me knew deep down inside that we would be in for a long ordeal, that there was much to be done. Again, I can't explain it except to say it was God's very real hand working in a situation that would bring Him glory.

The response was almost immediate. Looking back now, it seems almost as if God had been waiting to set His plan in motion. And once it was set in motion, it took off with a fury and power I never thought possible. I believe it is because I obeyed God immediately, without fully comprehending what He was asking me to do. He said: "Write." I wrote. It's a lesson I learned throughout this situation, a lesson I have carried with me to this day: When you feel God is telling you to do something, do it! Don't wait to understand it. Just do it. If you wait and try to have it make sense in your worldly perspective, you are wasting God's time. He knows what He wants to accomplish through you, even if you don't. I firmly believe my first unknowing act of obedience in sending that message had a part in the rapid-fire growth of God's mission through our child. What started out as a request for prayer because we were hurting would turn into something in which we were God's voice, reaching out and drawing others to Him. Through that we learned the most important lesson: If you are obedient to God, He can take even the worst of situations and make something good happen for His glory.

Jacob's Story

Within five hours of clicking "send," the prayers started to roll in, by e-mail, phone and visit, prayers that touched us so deeply it makes us well up with tears to think about, even to this day.

From a college friend, Beth, now living near Boston:

Oh, John. I am so sorry. You weren't at all prepared for this news, and that must be so hard. I'm sending lots and lots of prayers your way. God bless the Agliatas. Take care, my friend.

From a woman, Jen, who wrote freelance articles for the newspaper I was an editor for a few years back, someone who God had brought back into my life just two months before:

My heart aches for you, and I shed tears along with you. You two and your little one will be in my prayers. I wish I knew more to say to you. I will do anything at all to help you, and I will ask my friends and family to pray for you and Kix as well.

From a church friend, Chuck:

I've been praying for you. Now I'll pray for the three of you. I won't quote a lot of Scripture, but the Lord never said we won't go through dark times. What He did say is that we won't go through those dark times alone. Beyond prayer, what can we do to help share your burden?

When the sun went down ending August 30, 2000, we could already feel the prayers of those who would constantly and tirelessly rally around us—all three of us—in the months to come. To be sure, our souls ached with the uncertainty of what was to come, both tomorrow and thereafter but, seemingly out of nowhere, came a few certainties. One was that

34

A Journey of Faith

Carla and I had learned there was no doubt we would be going through this together. While we both dealt with it in different ways, we had already solidified ourselves as a team in facing whatever was to come. The second was that Carla and I had learned we would not be going through this alone. God was right there with us. One simple e-mail message had touched off a response I never expected and, unbeknownst to me, the situation we were facing was making its way around the country, to relatives of the original ten and to their relatives' relatives and friends and beyond.

Chapter Seven

Stepping Out on Faith

Sleep was hard to come by for me. While Carla slept deeply in our bed, I rested fitfully in a recliner, watching late-night television when I woke up from what amounted to brief interludes of shut-eye. Around 3 a.m. I quietly crept into our bedroom and into bed. Carla, as she had become accustomed to doing as she started to feel changes in her body, was on her left side, facing away from me. I curled up behind her in the classic spoons position that somehow always felt right, whether it was a time of great happiness, like our wedding night, or a time of great sadness, like the night her grandfather died. Now, in a time of unparalleled despair, I got as close to her as I could possibly get and reached my arm around her, placing my hand on her belly. I didn't know the particulars of pregnancy, but I knew that my hand was several inches from this tiny living thing that was our baby. There was such a feeling of unreality, that the doctors had to be wrong. How could there be a problem with something so tiny, something that could fit into the palm of the hand that I now used to reach out to our little Kix? With tears falling down my face and onto the back of Carla's shoulders, I prayed that God would work through my hand and heal our baby.

The following morning, like the previous afternoon when Carla had her blood drawn, showed us how meshing this horribly uncertain situation into our everyday lives would become something we would simply have to face. At around 5 a.m. I momentarily awoke and remembered I had an appointment to have my car serviced that morning. Should I cancel the appointment? If I did, what would I do at home but sit and wait for the phone to ring in hopes that it would be word of our appointments with specialists? Carla was resolute that she could do that, and that it wasn't a two person job.

So at 8 a.m. I found myself showering and putting on a pair of shorts and a T-shirt and driving to get the car's oil changed and tires rotated. It seemed almost laughable. Here we were in the midst of our worst nightmare and I was getting an oil change.

While I was waiting for the work to be done, Carla called me on my cell phone. Our angels had done their job. We now had our appointments for that afternoon in Cincinnati at Good Samaritan Hospital, about 40 minutes from our home. At those appointments we would find more of God's angels waiting for us.

There was little conversation between the two of us as we made the drive, save for one or the other pointing out a sign or turn as we found our way for the first time to a place I now can get to in my sleep. Though the words were few, I have never felt closer to Carla than I did at that time. A fierce protectionism swept over me, and as we walked into the hospital I held her

Jacob's Story

close to me, almost guarding her. I had grown used to being Carla's protector, though we never have faced any real danger. Call it chivalry, which, thanks to my father, is engrained in me, but I have lived my life with Carla under the theory that if you want to do any harm to her, you're going to have to kill me first. Now, here I was, knowing that she would be facing a hurt that I could do nothing about. In a loss for what to do, I see now, I ratcheted up that protective instinct to an almost smothering level.

We sat in the waiting room and were immediately struck by how different the world was. Around us sat a half dozen other pregnant women. One by one they were called back to the ultrasound room and returned with 3-by-5 pictures of their developing babies. Healthy babies. I wanted to cry out how unfair it was, how we had done everything right. From the second that we found out Carla was pregnant we'd been almost neurotic about keeping her away from cigarette smoke, paint fumes, alcohol, unhealthy food and anything that might affect our baby. How could this be happening when we'd tried so hard to do everything right?

It was doubly hard to keep our emotions in check when a girl who looked no older than 15 was called back for her ultrasound, her mother carrying her schoolbook bag and following a few steps behind. She returned a few minutes later carrying her baby's ultrasound picture, giggling like the schoolgirl she was, acting as if she had just been told which boy in sixth period had a crush on her. Resentment welled up in me and I couldn't contain myself.

"What is she going to pay her co-pay with? Her baby-sitting money?" I said to Carla, louder than a whisper, almost begging to be heard. It's something I regret now. If she heard me, I don't know. It wasn't until that night that God filled my heart with a reality that stuck with me throughout Carla's pregnancy.

That reality was simply this: I would not wish what was happening to Carla and me on anyone, whether it was my worst

38

A Journey of Faith

enemy or a 15-year-old girl. In fact, when I thought about it that night, I realized that Carla and I, because we were so solid as Christians and as a couple, were the perfect choice for this assignment. God knew we would not break and, perhaps more importantly, He knew we would not be afraid to be witnesses to what He was doing through us. There was no "why me?" from either of us. From the start of this we had an answer to that question even before it was asked. Why *not* us?

Mercifully, our wait for the doctor wasn't long. We were soon called back and made a long walk down a wide, sterile hallway into a room filled with monitors and other equipment. Inside was Dr. William Polzin. He was a wiry 6-foot-5 or so, and the first thought that struck me was "I wonder if he plays basketball?" He was wearing green surgical scrubs and cap that almost completely covered his close-cropped dark hair. He had a gray-speckled goatee and deep, soft, kind eyes that immediately set us at ease, at least as much as was possible under the circumstances. His handshake was firm and his mannerisms disarming, even to my fierce protectionism. I immediately had an overwhelming sense that Carla was in good hands.

After introductions and a quick review of the medical chart Dr. Bonar had faxed, he began to examine Carla, squirting the ultrasound goop as was done the day before. This time, however, thanks to technology costing in the hundreds of thousands of dollars per machine, our child came into clear view. The tears I had cried the day before came back, but unlike yesterday's, these were tears of joy. There, on the television screen in front of us, was our child, our Kix, looking like a little alien from *Close Encounters of the Third Kind*. There were his two little legs and a little head.

Dr. Polzin's exam was thorough. The longer it lasted, the more I focused on him, his eyes peering intently into the monitor as he searched for an explanation. Everything he did was with precision. Every movement he made had a purpose. Every twist of the wrist to move the ultrasound receiver seemed to be

39

Jacob's Story

exactly the right one to get the view he was looking for. When he finished, he sighed and, with equal precision, cleaned off the head of the receiver and placed it on its hook.

He turned to talk to us and I noticed how deeply he looked at Carla. While he spared the occasional glance for me, there was no doubt: She was his patient and he was talking to her. It was something I appreciated deeply.

In the e-mail update I wrote that night to a group that had in one day grown from 10 to 17 addresses, this is what I said:

> Hi all. Since this is the first time some of you are hearing of this, let me bring you all up to speed.
>
> Carla and I went for an ultrasound yesterday that revealed some bad things. Basically, there was no amniotic fluid and there was this big empty spot that the doctor thought was a distended bladder in the baby. So we went to a specialist today and here's what's going on:
>
> The reason there's no amniotic fluid is because it's all in the baby's bladder. At this point in any pregnancy, the amniotic fluid is made up mostly of urine. Our baby has a blockage that's not allowing him to expel urine. Thus, no fluid. The doctors have all been really straight with us and told us that this is a very serious complication and that it carries a ton of risk for the baby. Today we were given the choice of: terminate; do nothing and this baby would be born full term with kidneys that would probably be destroyed by what becomes poison (the urine sitting there); or take some proactive steps to try to see a) what's causing the blockage and b) if there's anything that can be done. We chose this option without hesitation.
>
> Tomorrow they will do three things. They will do what's called a CVS, which is where they take a sampling of the placenta and test it for chromosomal abnormalities. This can tell us if it's a chromosome thing. It can also tell us

A Journey of Faith

about the risks in any future children, if any. They will then drain the fluid from the baby's bladder, which is about four times the normal size. This will provide temporary relief for the baby. They will then test that urine as a baseline for future tests (more on that in a moment). The third thing they will do is infuse fluid into the placenta. This serves a few purposes. 1) It will provide some room for the baby and 2) it will give the doctors a better look at the organs and the baby himself.

Now, the fluid they infuse is basically worthless to the health of the baby. There's no way of replacing amniotic fluid. In fact, doctors really don't know where it comes from, seeing as how it is present even before the baby's renal system develops. So this fluid will be taken in and, like the urine now, won't be able to be expelled. They will do at least one more drain of the urine to compare it to the baseline. The point is to see if the kidneys are working or if this problem is being caused by kidneys that didn't develop right or have been damaged by the urine sitting there blocked.

What we're hoping for there, obviously, is that the kidneys are, indeed, OK, developed and functioning.

The risk, then, is that the lungs have been damaged. The lungs need the intake of fluid to develop properly. They also need the cushion the fluid provides to grow properly. Obviously, they've been taxed, so we don't know the damage, if any, to them.

If either the kidneys or the lungs are damaged beyond repair, the baby will not live long, if at all, when born.

So, my friends, I am telling you this: We need a miracle here. We need everything to go right. Last night and today before the tests, I prayed for a glimmer of hope, because yesterday I didn't see one. Today, I see that

Jacob's Story

glimmer. I don't know what it was, whether it was the prayers of those who knew of this yesterday or what, but something happened that gave me some strength today to be optimistic, even before that glimmer of hope presented itself. What I'm asking you is to keep praying. Pray hard. We need a miracle and we need you prayer warriors. I make no bones about it: This is God's world and He can do whatever he chooses and who am I to question His plans? But I darn sure am going to make sure He hears me that I want my baby to be OK. Please, pray hard, pray loud. JAMES 5:15-16.

As for Carla and me, we're doing OK, about as well as you can expect. Speaking for myself, I fluctuate between about three vastly different emotional states, all coming about two hours apart. It's better than them jamming together all at once like they were yesterday. Carla's hanging in there and is readying herself for what she knows might be some painful tests in the future. We appreciate and rely on all of your love, support and prayers. Thank you all so much.

John and Carla

Dr. Polzin gave us the news without mincing words. But his honesty was mixed with compassion in such a way that it took away that sometimes vast gap between doctor and patient. Perhaps it was because he showed concern for us on more than just a physical level. When he asked us how we were hanging in there, I said things that Carla instantly recognized as out of character for me.

"We're getting by on the prayers of our friends," I said. "We're both strong Christians and we trust God."

It was out of character because, though Christian, speaking of the Lord with anyone, let alone someone I had just met, was something I didn't normally do. Though I attended church

A Journey of Faith

fairly regularly and had deeply held Christian beliefs, I didn't share them with strangers very often, if at all. Now, the subject of God and Christianity hung out there like a circus performer on a high wire. It felt odd talking about God with a doctor, mostly, I realized, because I assumed that doctors couldn't possibly be Christians. After all, there is a big difference between where science says life comes from and where the Bible says life comes from and I couldn't see a way in which a doctor could traverse the territory between the two. On top of that, I had had several doctors during a college bout with mononucleosis who seemed to think they were God Himself, so perhaps it was experience that was influencing my thoughts.

Dr. Polzin, though, ended the silence by agreeing, saying, "Your faith is going to be important for you two now." He went on to talk a bit about his faith, its roots and how powerful it was for him.

Inside, I smiled. God had brought us a Christian doctor.

From there we were handed off to the geneticist, Kris Jarrett, an attractive young woman with dark brown eyes and brown hair that touched her shoulders. She had a reassuring smile and the demeanor of one who knew how to delicately, patiently but firmly handle parents-to-be who were in our situation. As we sat down, I immediately noticed the diplomas on the wall behind her. The words "Duke" and "South Carolina" set me at ease, giving me a feeling that we were in competent hands.

Kris walked us through our family histories, hunting for something that would tell us why this was occurring. Though littered with a disturbing amount of ailments, including Lyme disease, mononucleosis and an inherited blood disorder called Thalasemia, there were no genetic abnormalities in my family history.

As Carla answered Kris' questions, I began to feel uneasy. If there was something she could tell us, did we really want to know? What would the ramifications be to my relationship with Carla, my relationship to my family, if it were something on our

Jacob's Story

side of the family tree that was to blame? What if it was on hers? It seems almost silly now, if only because living through the experience has taught us both that it was never about blame, but at that moment I feared that if this could somehow be linked back to me or my side of the family, it would be all my fault. How could Carla live with me, I thought, if she knew that I was responsible for causing this to happen to our child?

Kris finished asking her questions and paused for a second.

"There doesn't seem to be anything that would indicate this would be genetic, but there's a lot to genetics that isn't on the surface," she said. "What I can tell you is that there is nothing glaringly obvious that would lead me to say 'This is it.'"

She told us about the genetic test Dr. Polzin would do that would give a more detailed look at the chromosomes. It would also tell us without a doubt if Kix was a boy or a girl.

"I will tell you this, though," Kris said. "This sort of situation happens almost exclusively in boys."

It was an odd time to smile, but I did.

A boy.

The response from my second e-mail was larger and as immediate as the first. It was amazing then, and even more amazing now, how different people reacted differently to the news from Dr. Polzin. Almost immediately, a small group of people who believed without a shadow of a doubt that Kix would be OK, that God would heal him, made themselves known. The first was Jen, the woman who had written free-lance articles for me in the past.

> I'm so excited and happy! There is hope here! I will keep praying for you, and so will my family and their friends. Keep being brave about it, and keep thinking it will all be okay. If you guys need anything after the tests, since

A Journey of Faith

I'm guessing Carla might not be feeling too well, please let me know.

Jen's offer to do whatever we needed was met by many others, as well. From our church friend, Chuck:

John and Carla,

There are a lot of people praying for the three of you. I prayed for you last night. I prayed for you at 4am this morning. And my normal morning devotional time was dedicated to you three. I'm not alone, there are a lot of others praying hard.

And in the first tangible example of how the message was starting to spread, the sister of my college friend, Beth, sent us this:

Hello Carla and John,

I am Beth's sister, Jenny. Beth has asked me to pray for your baby, and I will certainly do that. My husband and I have experienced the joy and sudden uncertainty of pregnancy. It is often difficult to understand God's works.

We will keep you in our prayers.

Carla and I have both been very fortunate in our lives in that we grew up with two-parent families where Mommy and Daddy loved each other and loved their children. We lived far from the poverty line and enjoyed life in the relative safety of the suburbs. But it wasn't until that night—amidst the uncertainty and sadness over Kix—that we really felt how blessed we were. As the e-mails kept coming in and the phone and doorbell kept ringing, we both realized we had never felt further from alone in our lives.

Chapter Eight

Beyond Bruises

That night we talked about what was to come tomorrow. The procedures Carla would be facing would involve inserting several very large needles into her abdomen, which was starting to become taut with the growing baby. To put it mildly, it wasn't going to tickle.

Carla was scared, to be sure, and she knew that the tests would hurt. Add onto that the frantic worrying about the health of the child that was a part of her and it would have been understandable if she were a basket case. Instead, she was the picture of composure and strength, something I would see again and again as the months crawled by.

That demeanor had been formed more than a decade earlier when, as a 13-year-old in the small town of Foristell, Missouri, she was faced with a life-threatening illness. We

A Journey of Faith

talked about the illness many times during our relationship. In fact, it was one thing she told me during the first discussion we had under a large oak tree when we decided to become an "us" during our freshman year in college. But it wasn't until this time in our lives that I realized how much that situation had molded her and that all the grace she showed in dealing with our child's situation got a test run during her childhood.

Carla and her parents first recognized something was wrong when she was running track. All of a sudden, she began getting an extraordinarily large number of bruises.

Her father, Marvin, recalls, "When one appeared there was always a reason why. Someone hit her arm or she missed the hurdle and hit her leg. The bruises just didn't appear from nowhere. There was a reason. While we were concerned, she had just had a physical in order to run track so we watched the bruises come and go. We even asked her to check with her track coach to see if he thought the bruises were unusual."

But things progressed beyond bruises. Carla, who by her own admission was a classic nerd in school, came home one early May day and told her parents she had fallen asleep during a movie in science class.

"I told my mom that the movie was really boring and that is why I fell asleep," Carla recalls.

However, her mom, Judy, wasn't fooled.

"That night I looked at her and thought she looked tired and had dark circles under her eyes," she said, "so I made a doctor's appointment for the next week, which was the earliest I could get."

That appointment would never be filled. Two days later, Carla for the first time in her life, asked to stay home from school. She had a fever of 100.4 and a slight sore throat, so the doctor agreed to see her that day.

"I don't remember a lot about the appointment," Carla said. "But I do remember getting my temperature taken. While I had the thermometer in my mouth, the doctor started telling

Jacob's Story

me they were going to draw blood. As he was explaining what the different tests would show, I passed out. I had never passed out before. I woke up with the doctor and my mom above me. After they took my blood, the tests showed every component of the blood was very low. Platelets that were supposed to be in the hundreds of thousands were only a couple of thousand. They immediately admitted me into the hospital."

Carla's parents remembered the moment the blood test results came back. "When the doctor and nurse appeared to give us the blood test results, the doctor didn't have to say a word. His white face said it all. What he did say was, 'We are admitting her to the hospital *now*.' If he said more, I don't remember," her mom said.

In interviewing Carla and her parents for their recollections on this time in their lives, what struck me again and again was Carla's spirit during the whole matter. Even when recalling it 13 years later, she still didn't focus on the fact that the doctors that night filled her and her parents in on all the possibilities, including various types of cancer. What she remembers speaks to who Carla is, someone who puts others before herself, even in the most trying times, someone who sees the small blessings in the midst of what many would consider a life-earthquake.

About the first night in the hospital, Carla remembers first and foremost not that she was facing a life-threatening diagnosis but rather that her two sisters, Dyan—two years her senior, and Sara—two years her junior, couldn't come visit her. Instead, they made a tape for her. "I thought that was the sweetest thing they could do!" she said.

A few days later, the diagnosis was in: aplastic anemia. Basically, her body had stopped making blood. Now, with technological advancements in medicine, it's a disease with a much higher cure rate. At that time, however, the cure—a bone marrow transplant—was a relatively new treatment but, without one, she would die. Both her parents and sisters had their blood

A Journey of Faith

tested to see if they would be a donor match. Parents had a 50 percent chance of being a match, doctors said. Sisters had a 25 percent chance.

Carla recalls the day her sisters came to see her after having their blood drawn. Again, I was amazed at where her focus was. It wasn't on the fact that this was truly her best hope to live. It was on others.

"They both walked into my room with Band-Aids on their arm. They looked kind of scared, but they were so sweet to me and said it was fine," she recalls.

Four days later they received the results.

"I remember the night the phone rang and it was the doctor telling us we had a match," Carla recalls. "Dyan matched as closely as two people can without being twins. We all were crying and jumping up and down and hugging and laughing all at once."

The doctor, however, reminded them that even with a perfect match the chance for success was just 70 percent. Carla would also have to face chemotherapy that would kill her immune system and leave her fatally susceptible to even the smallest of colds. Again, Carla's focus amazes me, especially considering she was just 13 years old.

"I just knew I was going to be in that 70 percent," she said.

Carla was placed in a sterile room on the bone marrow transplant floor at Barnes Hospital in St. Louis. No one could see her without being first taken to the washroom to scrub their hands and put on a gown and mask. The biggest worry for Carla during this time was not the chemicals that were about to be dripped into her body, the major illness that had shut down blood production or the 30 percent chance this bone marrow transplant would fail. On those topics she was very serene. Rather, it was something else that brought her to tears.

"The doctor said that because my immune system would be wiped out I'd have to miss a year of school. My mom and I burst out in tears at the thought of that! I remember the doctor

Jacob's Story

leaving the room to give us a few minutes to compose ourselves and think about everything. When she came back in, she calmed us down by suggesting that maybe I could have a tutor so I wouldn't be a year behind. I could just picture all my friends graduating a year before me and I didn't like the idea of that at all. But then we got back to the task at hand...saving my life."

In fact, her parents recall her crying just four times during the whole ordeal. "And two of those times were because she would miss school for so long," her dad remembers.

After three days of chemotherapy, Dyan's bone marrow was dripped into Carla's body. Again, Carla's focus was not on her chances for survival. Rather, it was on others.

"That was more painful for Dyan than for me," she says. "She had anesthesia to completely knock her out and in surgery she had holes drilled into her hip bones and her bone marrow was extracted. I got Dyan's bone marrow through an IV. It took less than an hour to drip into me. I remember it smelling like Chinese food."

From there, it was a waiting game to see if Dyan's bone marrow would take and spur Carla's body into making blood again. While her life hung in the balance, Carla's focus shows her other-centered thinking and her ability to keep her own trials in perspective.

"My parents got to meet family members of other patients on the floor. It turns out I had it the easiest. Almost everyone else on the floor had cancer and needed radiation."

It was then that Carla's hair started to fall out from the chemotherapy. Soon, she was bald. Her parents offered to get her a wig, but Carla would have none of that. As her dad recalls, she said "No, that wouldn't be natural."

Even during what her parents call her darkest hour, Carla was the one lifting other's spirits. "She told us, like the song that was popular then, don't worry, be happy," her dad recalls.

Carla's 30-day blood work showed the results her family had been praying for. Her bone marrow was making blood

A Journey of Faith

again. This meant she could go home. Her parents recalled how bittersweet it was for them and for Carla, saying goodbye to the other families on the floor when they knew that many of their loved ones were not going to be going home ever again.

Carla recalls her own happiness at being home, but again, her recollection is decidedly other-centered.

"I remember feeling bad for Dyan because I got all the attention and she was the one who had to go through the physically painful stuff," Carla said. "I pretty much got to lay in bed and watch TV!"

Though there were a few minor bumps in the rest of her road to recovery, Carla rebounded faster than expected and missed only nine weeks of school, which she quickly made up. In 1992, she graduated with the rest of her class. To this day, the bond between her and Dyan is extremely evident. They still weep when the song "Wind Beneath My Wings" comes on, and there is a closeness there that can't be described. It often goes unspoken because of who they both are, but it's touching to see.

As Carla faced another daunting medical situation, this time for the baby that grew inside of her, I knew that much of how she was handling it was formed 13 years before. Lying in bed with her that night, I realized how truly awe-inspiring it was to say that the person I admired most in the world was my wife.

Chapter Nine

On Prayers and Needles

The morning was filled with painful irony. Not only were we getting ready for the medical procedures, we were packing suitcases and coolers for a trip to Tennessee. I had booked the Labor Day getaway to a mountain cabin in Gatlinburg before we found out Carla was pregnant. My thinking was that if we hadn't gotten pregnant despite all our "trying," it would be the perfect change of scenery to provide us with inspiration to "try" harder. If we had gotten pregnant, then it would be the perfect romantic getaway for us to relax, look at the beautiful scenery and enjoy the last vacation we had before our lives were taken over by diapers, feedings, crying and spit-up. As it turned out, the mini-vacation high up in the mountains would serve to unite us spiritually for the months ahead.

My stomach was churning as we drove to the hospital. Part of it was from the thought of the procedures themselves.

A Journey of Faith

The risks to Carla were minimal, but the risks to Kix were a bit more. Three needles would be inserted through Carla's abdomen. The first would scrape material from the wall of the uterus to be tested for chromosomal abnormalities, such as Down Syndrome. The second needle would be inserted through Carla's abdomen, into the uterus, into Kix and into his bladder. The backed-up fluid would be drained to relieve the pressure and to be tested to see how well the kidneys were functioning. This procedure was called a bladder tap. The third needle would be inserted into the uterus into the tiny amount of remaining empty space to inject fluid around Kix to give him room to move around and also to help with differentiation on the ultrasounds. Any move by Dr. Polzin in the wrong direction could cause premature labor; plus, the stress of a needle in Kix's body could simply be too much for him.

But those risks were small. As tough as it was to admit to Carla what was really causing my stomach to churn, her knowing glace and probing "What's wrong?" gave me no choice: The thought of the needles, I told her, was getting to me. Not only would she have to worry about the sticks, but she was probably going to have a passed-out husband on her hands as well.

"You don't have to go in," she said. "I'll have them come get you when it's done."

I knew what I should have said. I should have said, "No, honey, I will be there by your side. I won't fail you." But I didn't. Instead, I said the loaded "Are you sure?" which pretty much locked her into saying, "Yes, I'm sure."

The plan was set. Carla would go in and face three needles the length of my forearm and I would wait outside the door until it was done. It was a good plan, one that certainly settled my stomach momentarily. The only problem was that it wasn't God's plan.

Carla was taken back into the same exam room we had been in the day before and I sat on a bench outside the door. Nurses and assistants came in and out of the room as they

Jacob's Story

prepped her for the procedure. It was then that God reached me.

"What are you doing? Why are you out here while she's in there?"

It was tough to recognize the voice, but it was extremely audible in my head. It was a combination of what I picture God sounding like, coupled with my father's and grandfather's voice. I thought most about my grandfather. Rosario "Rocky" Agliata was born in Italy and ran away from an abusive stepfather as a teenager, taking a boat that resembled the Titanic to the New World where he was met by his older brother, Mike. He was an uneducated but proud man whose chest swelled when he talked about surviving the Great Depression on a janitor's salary without ever receiving any form of government assistance. He and my grandmother raised my father with a ton of pasta and an equally large serving of morals, values and work ethic. He was a man of principle and raised my father as a man of principle. His death from cancer and pneumonia when I was 13 marked the first time I ever saw my father cry.

It was mostly his heavily Italian accented voice I was hearing as I sat outside the room where doctors were preparing to use my wife as a human pincushion, a voice that was chastising me for not living up to my obligation as a husband to Carla and a father to Kix. My place was in there, not out here.

Without any hesitation, I got up and made my way into the exam room. I locked eyes with Carla, lying on the exam table with her shirt pulled up, belly exposed. She gave me a smile of satisfaction, a smile that told me she was relieved I had done the right thing. Without a word, I pulled up a chair beside her bed and grabbed her hand. The room grew quiet as Dr. Polzin and the nurses began. Being in the room was one thing; looking at the needles was something entirely different. With Carla's hand firmly in mine, I put my head down to silently prayed:

"Dear God, please be with Carla right now. Please take away the pain. Guide the doctor's hand and be with him. And,

A Journey of Faith

please, protect Kix. Keep the needles from hurting him. And thank you for sending Grandpa's voice to me."

Before I knew it, the tests were over. Carla was smiling. When Dr. Polzin asked her how it had been, she responded, "It hardly hurt at all."

"Thank you, God," I said silently.

Dr. Polzin then continued his exam. In an e-mail to the prayer list, which was now up to 27 addresses, I wrote:

> Hi all. First off, let me tell you that we have been so amazed by all your prayers and warm thoughts that you've shared with us. I know I can't know for certain when you all are praying, but Carla and I have both mentioned that at certain times we feel stronger than others, and maybe that's when you all are praying, or maybe just one of you is praying. Whatever the case, we appreciate the thoughts, prayers, messages and calls.
>
> Let me update you on how things are going. Friday, Carla bravely faced three very big needles. The first one was a CVS test that will see if this problem is being caused by any genetic abnormalities. The second drained the fluid that is blocked in the baby's bladder. Modern medicine is such a miracle from God, to think about what they did on Friday. The third was an infusion of saline solution to give the doctor's a clearer view of the baby's anatomy and also to give the baby room to move around (which he immediately did. Very cute!).
>
> The only new info we got on Friday was that the doctor said the baby's kidneys, clearer with the saline solution to differentiate things, were a bit white and fuzzy. This isn't a good thing, most likely. White means damage, caused by the urine backed up there, which no one knows how long it's been there. Of course, this doesn't tell us if it's damage or malformation (meaning the kidneys didn't develop

55

Jacob's Story

right) or, if it's damage, to what degree that damage is. So there's still, well, everything is still up in the air.

We are going back on Tuesday. At that time they will drain the baby's bladder again and then compare that fluid against that which they took Friday. That will give them an indication if the kidneys are functioning at all or to what degree. They also might do another saline solution infusion, for the reasons mentioned above.

For someone like me whose job as a journalist is to nail down the facts and who thrives on certainties, leaving that doctor's office and heading to Tennessee without anything definite was difficult. God had begun teaching me a strong lesson on patience, a lesson long overdue in my life.

For the first 26 years, my life seemed like one big rush. High school was a means to college which was a means to the career I'd been set on since I was 16—journalism. My first job was a means to show what I was capable of in an effort to climb the ladder into management, which, when I found myself there at a very young age, was a means to further my pursuit of an even better job. Rarely in those rushed journeys did I stop to look at the scenery, to appreciate where I was coming from and where I was headed. Never was I content to be in a situation where there weren't some certainties about the direction things were going. Now, there were no certainties, no clear path, and I was learning quickly that I'd better learn to like life that way because that's how it was going to be.

The drive to Tennessee was emotional. As our car steamed south, Carla, mentally and physically spent, napped in the passenger seat and my mind drifted for what seemed like hours on end. I kept thinking back to the view on the television screen after Dr. Polzin inserted the fluid around our Kix, the way his little legs moved, almost as though he were saying, "It's about time I got some room in here."

56

Could he feel the needle that pierced his body and went into his bladder? Did it hurt him? Does he know what's going on? Does he know that his mommy and daddy are trying to help him and don't want to hurt him? Is he scared?

Carla awoke next to me to find tears running down my cheeks from behind my sunglasses. Seeing Kix move had made him so real to me. There he was, right there on that television screen, moving around independently of any movement Carla made. The irony struck me deeply. He was so independent in some ways, yet he was totally helpless, relying on us to do the right thing while being faced with decisions that threatened to overwhelm us. Ultimately, it was the thought of him having feelings and emotions and experiencing pain that had been too much for me to handle right then. It was undeniable: Kix was a person. He was my child. Traveling down Interstate 75 with my unshaven face moist from the tears, I vowed that I would never give up on Kix until God decided he had breathed his last breath.

The long weekend in Tennessee was one of the oddest weekends of my life. The range of emotions in those three days was so vast that it was draining. The lows were to be expected. We spent the first evening on the couch, in each other's arms, crying. It was the highs that took us by surprise.

They would come out of nowhere, laughter and joking **and** smiles. As we drove around one afternoon through the hokey tourist strip of Gatlinburg and up into Great Smokey National Park, we goofed around like high school kids.

And then, suddenly, we'd remember. Our Kix was in trouble. With that remembering came guilt. "Was I really just laughing when there is something so seriously wrong with my child? What kind of father am I? What kind of *person* am I?" And soon after those feelings started the lows would return

Jacob's Story

stronger than before. With each cycle the extremes were further and further apart, and it gave me the impression that the world was truly out of control and there was nothing I could do about it. We went through these cycles while doing whatever we could to enjoy our vacation, going out to eat, shopping, playing pool, grilling hot dogs. We also did something we'd never done before—pray together.

It was odd that we'd been married more than three years, were deeply committed to God but yet had never prayed together. Sure, we'd said grace before meals, but we had never sat down together and spoken our prayers to God. The only reason, I guess, is that we both weren't the stereotypical "good pray-ers." When it came time to pray, we'd certainly bow our heads and fervently send our petitions to God, but we did so silently. In that mountain cabin, Carla made the suggestion to pray aloud together. The sun had fallen and night had come quickly. Rain fell steadily outside and beat a rhythmic pattern on the roof. For the first time since we'd arrived in Tennessee, our unconscious efforts to constantly be doing something had run into a wall and we were left sitting alone with our thoughts. And it just so happened to catch us both at the lowest of the lows.

When Carla said, "Can we pray?" I agreed without hesitation. Together, alone with God, we prayed, her hand resting on mine, which rested on her tender belly. It was a soul-revealing, tear-soaked prayer filled with our deepest fears and our greatest hopes. We confessed our sins and asked God to hear us and to heal our baby. We prayed for strength to face the medical procedures and emotional roller coaster, and we both told God that we trusted Him to work His will in this situation.

As I wrote to the people on the e-mail prayer list:

We have gotten very specific in what we're praying for. Both of us believe that this, like everything else, is truly out of our hands. It's God's plan, and we might not like

A Journey of Faith

it or agree with it, but it's not up to us to decide. Still, that doesn't mean we aren't going to pray to God for exactly what we want. Yes, it's up to God, but we are going to pray hard for things to turn out in a way that will bring us this tiny miracle baby to hold and raise and send off to college and into life.

The interesting thing was that from the moment we prayed that prayer together, the lows were never again as low as they were before. United before Him, God had heard us and from that day on was a constant source of strength ministering to our wounded hearts, lifting us up just that little bit on the worst of days and making sure we had our share of smiles as we faced what we had to face.

Chapter Ten

The Kindness of Friends

If Tennessee had provided even the smallest escape for us from reality, coming back home brought it all back. There were doctor's appointments ahead filled with more procedures and, at best, just a small ray of hope. There were choices to be made that we both felt entirely unprepared for, choices we couldn't fathom having to make.

Also waiting for us back home was an increasingly large group of concerned people ready to carry our cross in any way possible. Our e-mail boxes overflowed with messages and the first of many cards began to fill our mailbox. There were other acts of kindness that, in the midst of everything, made us smile, take a step back and re-evaluate how we look at the world around us.

It started with a simple request: Food. As I wrote in an e-mail update:

A Journey of Faith

We could really use some help with some meals. No matter what is going to happen in the future, right now, Carla is pregnant and needs to be feeding herself and that baby well. With all the doctor's visits to Cincinnati and the mental and emotional toll this is taking, eating a balanced lunch and dinner has become a challenge. She and the baby need their fruits, veggies and good main dishes. So if any of you can help there, we'd sure be appreciative. Reheatable things would be great.

Within eight hours of sending that message, we had a refrigerator and freezer so full of food, we couldn't fit any more in. Without hesitation, people prepared and delivered plates full of nutritious and tasty food. The most touching were the five bags of groceries brought by two Miami University college students, Andrea and Erik. Andrea was editor of the student paper for which I was advisor and, during the course of work, we'd begun talking about our personal lives, including her pending nuptials with Erik and my pending bundle of joy in Kix. When she heard about our need, she and Erik went to the local grocery store and brought us enough food to last for weeks. What was so touching to us was that we had been college students not too long ago and remembered how strained our finances had been. They had little, yet they gave so much.

That night I wrote to my parents and sister:

Subj: The kindness of our friends...

Hi parents and sister. I just wanted to tell you about the kindness of our friends, which has left us in tears tonight. Less than, what, seven or eight hours after I sent my update message to people, our freezer and fridge are stuffed with reheatable meals and groceries from our friends. Ted and Monica brought six meals. Andrea (the *High Street Journal* editor and a really kind person) and her boyfriend, Erik (who delivers the HSJ and writes a column) came over soon after with a bunch of groceries, including milk, fruit salad, lunch meat, potato salad and chocolate for Carla! These are college kids with a college kid-sized bank account spending their money and their time on us. It just amazes me how kind people can be.

I felt my child kick for the first time today. A little boot to Carla's belly. I don't want to believe that God would let me feel that and not let me ever hold that child in my arms. I trust in God and in His way, that He is the one who makes the plans, and I know that God's plan sometimes causes humans pain, for a higher good. But I don't want to believe that God would let me feel my child like that and take him from me without letting me hold him at least once.

The next week was a blur of doctor's appointments. Not only were we facing appointments at Good Samaritan for the more specialized treatment with Dr. Polzin, but we were told to keep our regular appointments with Dr. Bonar. They would be sharing information, and having each one checking on the other's conclusions gave us some measure of comfort.

The day after we returned from Tennessee, we made the drive down to Good Samaritan again. It was a tense car ride, as we would receive the results from the first bladder tap. Unspoken between the two of us was the thought that maybe, just maybe, the results would show that things were fine. The belief that God could do that was strong in us and in others who had e-mailed us from near and far. Myla, a college friend who lives in Colorado, wrote:

A Journey of Faith

Carla and John,

Just want you to know that you and, of course, the baby
are in my prayers. I have also told my network of prayer
warriors as well. We are believing for a miracle. As someone who has been on the receiving end of a miracle and
who has also seen firsthand miracles done for others, I
truly know that nothing is impossible for God. I am
believing for total restoration and healing in your baby.
Know that I am here for you and will continue to pray
without ceasing. There is definitely a power that comes
when people pray in one accord.

Some would say it is foolish to hold on to such hope when
all the medical evidence tells you otherwise. If you take a step
back from the reasons we hold our faith, it is, indeed, hard to
argue with quantifiable medical test results when the only
defense is the belief in an unseen trinity that no one can seem to
truly understand or explain. The very premise of faith, I thought
as we drove to Cincinnati that day, is flimsy if you try to justify it
with anything that makes rational sense to one who believes only
in what can be experienced with the five senses. But, I realized,
the fact that so many people do share such similar forms of a
common faith proves to me there is reason to believe. And
beyond that, what we were directly experiencing in answer to our
prayers for strength told me God was real and listening. That
was what was in my head and heart as we followed the nurse
back into the exam room and waited for Dr. Polzin.

Again, as would become customary, we didn't have to wait
long. Dr. Polzin came in and immediately expressed concern not
only for Carla's physical well-being, but also our mental well-
being with the strain of the situation.

"How are you guys holding up?" he asked in a caring and
soothing tone.

"Hanging in there," Carla said.

"Tired," I added. "But we're really leaning on each other."

Jacob's Story

"That's good. It really is," he said. He turned his attention to a manila folder and opened it up. "We got some test results back and I guess I can say it's not good. These are the tests of kidney function, from the bladder tap. The values that should be high are low and the values that should be low are high. What does that mean? It means that kidney function appears to be impaired to some degree. We'll do another bladder tap and compare that to these results to see exactly what the case is and whether it's even worth trying to fix the bladder obstruction."

The words were like daggers to my heart. The hope that I had held that God had heard our prayer to heal Kix disappeared. It was hard not to be bitter. Had He heard? Did He care? Why didn't He fix this? In the face of such bad news, it was hard to keep the perspective that sometimes bad things to us are good things for God and His glory and kingdom.

"We don't have all of the results back, but my opinion is that they won't be much different from what we're seeing here," Dr. Polzin continued. "And we still don't have the results back on the genetic screening, but that should be back by the end of the week. I wish I had something positive to tell you, but I just don't."

He paused and gave us time to digest what we had just heard. God hadn't given us the miracle we wanted. At least, not yet. And it didn't look like medical science was going to be much of a help. Where did that leave us? It was hard to comprehend that we could have knowledge of a problem but not be able to fix it. Perhaps that is the typical response for a guy—to want to be able to fix things—but it was just so hard to accept that we couldn't do anything to make this better.

After we'd had a few moments, Dr. Polzin gave us the agenda for the appointment. He'd do another ultrasound and take measurements of the baby and see how much of the fluid he had inserted Friday remained. Eventually, we knew, Kix would swallow that fluid and his cushion would disappear

A Journey of Faith

again. If necessary, the doctor would insert more fluid and also do another bladder tap.

Carla laid back and Dr. Polzin gooped up her belly, seemingly larger every day. He put the receiver on her and, within moments, there was our baby. There was still some fluid around him, and as we watched he moved his arms and legs and squirmed a bit. Carla and I smiled. There was the reason why we would not give up hope. There was the reason why we wouldn't take the seemingly easy road and just "end" the problem. He might have a major developmental problem, but there on that screen, clear as day, was his tiny heart beating. He moved independently from Carla. He was in every sense, right then and there, our child.

The needles, which only a few days earlier had been enough to make me feel as if I were going to vomit, were as threatening as a kitten now. Fear of the unknown was no longer a hindrance. All that mattered now was just supporting Carla as much as I could. God had changed me so significantly, strengthening me in just a matter of days. That said, I still didn't look up from the time the needles were brought into the room until the time they were disposed of in the hazardous waste container. In the interim, Kix's swollen bladder had been drained and Carla's uterus had been filled with fluid. She made it through without so much as a whimper.

That night, I wrote an e-mail update to a list of addresses that had grown to 40. After updating them on the medical situation, I wrote:

> We are both feeling a tremendous sense of helplessness and hopelessness right now. It is tough to keep getting our hopes up only to have doors slammed in our face. I am resolute in the belief that this is God's plan, but that doesn't stop me from really disagreeing with how He's taking things right now. I pray that He doesn't find me disobedient in His eyes.

Jacob's Story

We will be going back either Thursday or Friday (most likely the latter) for a third bladder tap. The results from the genetic test from last Friday might be back by then too, which could tell us the cause of this all or it could tell us nothing. The fluid from that third bladder tap will be compared against the first two to see if there is any trend to the values they're looking at getting better.

Even in this hopelessness, immediately following hearing what the doctor said about these tests, I ask you... PLEASE KEEP PRAYING. GET SPECIFIC WITH GOD. WE NEED GOOD TEST RESULTS. WE NEED STRENGTH. WE NEED SOME GOOD NEWS. SOME HOPE. WE NEED THESE VALUES THAT THEY LOOK AT TO SHOW THEM SOMETHING THAT SAYS THERE'S STILL A FIGHTING CHANCE. WE NEED KIDNEYS THAT SOMEHOW REPAIR THEMSELVES OR SHOW THAT THEY REALLY AREN'T THAT DAMAGED OR DAMAGED AT ALL. WE NEED NOTHING SHORT OF A MIRACLE.

Thank you all for your love and thoughts and prayers. You all mean so much to us.

Another restless night was filled with a thousand questions we didn't ask the doctors. It amazed me how in the intensity of the moment we could forget so many things that only later stick out in their urgency. The biggest question that kept running through my mind that night as I tried unsuccessfully to sleep was this: What is going to happen if what the doctors think is going to happen actually happens? In my mind, the question had a disturbing level of acceptance to it. It was admitting to a large degree the correctness of what medical science was telling us. On one level, that racked my soul. Was I being faithless? In this seemingly illogical acceptance of the situation,

A Journey of Faith

was I showing God that I didn't believe He could or would heal our baby? Or was this all about leftover disappointment from having our hopes dashed by Dr. Polzin and the test results? But on a deeper level I felt that precisely because the acceptance of such a horrible diagnosis was illogical, I was feeling God's comforting hand helping me to begin to see and face reality with both eyes open and as unafraid as possible.

By the time morning rolled around, I knew I couldn't wait until Friday to find out the answer to this question. Carla called Dr. Polzin's office, and within an hour he called back.

"What does this mean, then? What if what you're thinking is happening really is happening?" she asked.

"Well, it means that your baby's kidney functions would most likely be, um, incompatible with life. It would all depend on how things go with the other tests, but the goal would be to take the pregnancy as long as we could. In situations where there has been a low-fluid environment, the mothers typically deliver early and lung function might already be somewhat impaired from being in the low-fluid environment, so it would be helpful for you to carry as long as possible. And then if your baby is born alive, he might live a few hours."

Incompatible with life? Low-fluid environment? Might live a few hours? As Carla explained the conversation to me the words and phrases spun through my head like a tornado. On an intellectual level, it all made sense. If what the doctors were seeing was true, our baby's kidneys could not do the job they needed to do for him to live. Having spent time in a low-fluid environment, where the sucking in of amniotic fluid for some reason unknown even to doctors is key to lung development, he might not be able to breathe well enough to live and in two hours or so after birth, he would die. Intellectually, I got it. Emotionally, it was incomprehensible.

Almost immediately after Carla hung up the phone, I felt pulled toward my computer keyboard. Ten minutes later, I had typed out an e-mail update to the list of family, friends and

Jacob's Story

strangers. By the time my fingers stopped moving, I had to re-read what I'd just written. When I did, I realized I had no clue at the time what I was writing. With a sense of awe that made my stomach feel like it does on a roller coaster just as it begins its first big drop, I put my head in my hands and cried.

> We talked to the doctor today again to ask him some questions. We have an appointment Friday at 9 a.m. for a third bladder tap and then we'll talk to him about this whole deal.
>
> "The whole deal" meaning this: Based on the test results we're getting back, our baby's kidneys are most likely not functioning. They don't and won't know if this is what led to the blockage or if the blockage damaged the kidneys beyond function. There will be one more bladder tap, as I said, and then we will discuss the possibility of putting the shunt in, the possibility of doing more "heroic" things. Two things on this: If there is no kidney function, they most likely won't do anything because nothing will help. And if they will do something, it has to be balanced against the risk it puts Carla under, meaning surgery, increased risk of miscarriage, increased risk of infections, etc.
>
> So if things keep going as they are, and the doctor believes they most likely will, Carla will continue to be pregnant. The baby, healthy in every other way they can tell (head size, limb formation, weight, size, etc.) will continue to grow and develop. We'll feel the baby kick, see the baby move inside of her, go to childbirth classes and all the rest. Carla will go into labor, possibly early because of the lack of fluid, and the baby will be born. His lungs will most likely not be able to support life for much more than an hour. If they can, his kidneys will not support life for much longer than that. He will die

68

and an autopsy will determine whether this was a freak one-in-a-million thing or whether this was something that will affect us if we try to have another child. It will also determine if the kidneys never formed right or if they were damaged by the blockage.

We are really clinging to the belief that there is some plan in all of this for God, something that we may never see. But I find it really hard to believe that it is not anything but cruel that I am going to have to sit here and watch my wife grow gloriously more and more pregnant, have to tell those who don't know what's going on that yes, we're pregnant and pretend we're happy so as not to make them feel bad for innocent inquiries, await that "time" when labor hits knowing that we're not going to be bringing our child home. Carla is going to have to feel this baby growing and moving inside her, deal with all the problems of third-trimester pregnancy, go through the pain of labor and then be there when our child dies. Where is God's love in that? Where's the plan in that? I am really trying to see it and I believe it is there. I just never thought there would be such a long and deep valley put before us. I was ready when we got pregnant for a miscarriage, especially early on. I knew it could happen. Several of you have felt that pain yourselves and I am in no way diminishing how hard that must be. But from now until January, we have to descend into that valley, get to know our child in every way a pregnant couple gets to know their child, all the while KNOWING that the doctors say there is no chance he will live. Only God can provide the strength for us to face that.

Do I still believe a miracle can happen? Without a doubt. God certainly has more power than the doctors. God gives the doctors their power. Things can always change

Jacob's Story

because God can lead them that way. We go to the doctor again this afternoon for what was supposed to be our "normal" monthly check-up but is now so much more. Things could change even there.

I just can't help but see some cruelty in this and wonder where that comes from and how to face it and beat it.

God will strengthen us and your prayers and constant support will strengthen us. Others have surely faced more than this and survived. It's just the constant, long-lasting pain—that will be always there and quite visible from now until January—that is so hard to face, that is so THERE during our weaker moments.

Again, friends and family, thank you for your heartfelt responses and care of us. We will never, ever forget what you have done and are doing to help us.

I look back at what I wrote that day and I see how honest my grappling with God was. It wasn't disrespectful to the Creator of the universe, but it was honest in saying, "I don't see how You're working. I don't get it. I want to get it because not getting it really is too much. But You know what, God? Even if I don't get it, I'll still follow You. I'll still do everything You ask of me in this situation. I'll still write e-mail updates when You tell me. I'll still be a witness for You in this situation whenever You give me the opportunity. And if there are other ways You want me to work in this situation, I'll do it. Whatever it is. There might be a lot ahead of us, things that alone I know I could not face. And I am not exactly happy about the fact that You have either put this path or allowed this path to be put before us, but You know what? No matter what, I will be Your servant."

The responses were touching. From my cousin Kathy:

A Journey of Faith

Hi John and Carla,

I just checked in this morning. I had spoken to Aunt Nadine and she told me you guys had the first wave of tests done and had gone away for the weekend. That was a good thing to do. Sometimes trying to keep as normal a routine as possible is very helpful. I am sure by the time you read this you will have completed another exhausting day of tests. I cannot imagine how anxious you must feel before each of these. Whatever happens, whatever will be, keep talking, letting it out, sharing the fear and the hope. No matter what happens, this will change your life in so many ways, and it will make you stronger as a couple, in faith, and in love. There is nothing more important than love, faith and family, and you have all those. We all feel helpless, but we are praying for you to be strong and able to deal with what will come, and for a miracle. I believe in miracles. Just remember, you are surrounded by love and prayer, and that will have to sustain you through the tough times. Hang in there. We are all thinking of you.

From Andrea, the Miami University student and college newspaper editor who had filled our refrigerator with food:

Hello John and Carla! How are you holding up? I know, stupid question, but one has to ask it!

Every time you send me another email, I notice the list of its recipients getting longer and longer! It is nice to see the community of love and support surrounding you!

I got this email at 4 Wednesday morning when I got home from the paper and it was a shock. Please hold on to that glimmer of hope that you have. I know that I will be.

71

Jacob's Story

I can understand your feelings of helplessness and hopelessness right now, I know that's how I would feel anyway. Both of you amaze me in your strength and willingness to put the whole situation in God's hands, whatever the test results say. That unfailing faith is what will get you through this! Not many people would be that willing to recognize God's role in this type of situation; I'm not too sure I could be that strong!

I am praying harder than ever for all three of you. I don't tell you that to make myself look good, but I know that some of your strength is coming from well wishes so I want to give you as many as I can.

I'm praying hard, every day. I know that it is hard to see right now, but this baby is a huge blessing, so just think of the blessings once he is born! He is very special!

Please continue to let me know of anything else you need or want. Are you still pretty stocked as far as food? Don't hesitate to call.

From my college friend Beth, in Boston:

John, Well, if you ever had any doubts about your writing abilities, I can assure you that your thoughts are coming across very clearly. I can actually feel your agony. I know there are no magic words, so the best I can do is a few phrases that I fall back on when times are tough:

1. "God never gives us more than we can handle together (with Him)." And He must think a lot about your (you and Carla's) ability to handle things right now because He sure is asking a lot of you guys. You are certainly bearing one of the biggest crosses I've ever seen. I know it's a little different because you are anticipating that Carla will carry the baby to full term, but I know one thing that my sister and her husband found consolation in when they lost

A Journey of Faith

their baby...they referred to that child as the little angel whom God sent to say they COULD get pregnant (since they'd been trying without success for awhile). That's all his little mission was, and once he delivered that message, it was his time to go. But he lives on in their hearts and the little angel who came to deliver good news.

2. "We cannot direct the wind but we can adjust our sails." I know you guys are struggling so hard to keep doing that and I just want to encourage you to keep that up. It's a lot like one of my favorite passages from the Bible, called the Serenity Prayer, which you probably know, but it goes like this: "God grant me the serenity to accept the things I cannot change, the courage to change the things I can, and the wisdom to know the difference." Hang in there, John. It won't be this hard forever. As always, my prayers are with you guys.

Chapter Eleven

A Lifetime with My Boy

Friday's 9 a.m. appointment was filled with the same nerves from two mornings ago. Though it wasn't as strong as before, my thought that maybe, just maybe, God had completely healed Jacob made me anxious with anticipation.

Before we even had a chance to sit down in the waiting room, Kris Jarrett, the geneticist, met us in the hallway and ushered us into her office to talk about the results of the genetic screening. She showed us pictures of Kix's actual chromosomes and pointed out that there were no apparent defects.

"I guess you could call it good news," she said hesitantly. "It's not chromosomal, which means there's a dramatically smaller chance this would ever happen again in future pregnancies." Then she quickly added. "Of course, that doesn't change how things are right now with this pregnancy."

Then she said: "And, by the way, you see these two chromosomes here? It's a boy."

Kix. A boy. I smiled. Jacob Alexander Agliata.

Kris then handed us off to Dr. Polzin. As I wrote in an e-mail update that evening:

> Hi all. It's kind of amazing how things go.
>
> We went in Friday not expecting anything positive, but still praying for total healing. If you'd drawn a line down the center of a page and put all the positives on one side and all the negatives on the other, you'd have one lopsided page. Well, yesterday we got a few small checkmarks on the positive side. First of all, the chromosome test came back normal, meaning there's nothing like Down syndrome or spina bifida or anything like that. Second, we found out through those chromosome tests that IT'S A BOY. Jacob Alexander Agliata. Third, we got some cute ultrasound pictures, in which he looks like he's smiling at us. Fourth, the baby's kidneys are, indeed, producing some urine. And fifth, the doctor for the first time could see some of what he called the kidney pelvis structure. He hadn't been able to see that before.
>
> The kidneys still don't look normal. Kidneys are supposed to be segmented, much like a cut-up pie, with individual pieces. This is why people can sometimes have part of a kidney removed. Our baby's kidneys don't look like that. There's not that distinction. So that's not good.
>
> They did another bladder tap, which Carla again faced bravely. They also infused more fluid to help the baby move around a bit and to give the doctors a better look at things. Carla and Jacob both came through this fine.

Jacob's Story

SO, now we wait again. Monday afternoon should bring us the remaining test results, and then we'll see what we can do, if we can do anything.

We both have gotten to the point where we accept that this is probably not going to be good, while we still pray for a miracle and ask you all to keep praying for a miracle. I am to the point where I realize that I have a lifetime to spend with my son... his lifetime, however long that might be. And that lifetime includes right now. So I'm not going to ignore my wife's growing belly. I'm not going to shy away from touching her when she says that baby is kicking (which he's getting good at!). I'm going to enjoy every minute I have with Jacob. It's his lifetime and I'm his daddy and I'm going to be a good daddy to him for as long as God lets me.

Of course it's going to be difficult and of course it's going to be really hard sometimes. But is there any other good choice in this? Should I ignore my wife? Not look at her and her belly? Not treat my son as my son for as long as I can? I know some might not understand what we're doing and what I'm saying, but to me this seems to be the obvious way to go, given our beliefs and the circumstances.

We continue to pray for a miracle and we continue to pray that God will use our child as the miracle baby, to show to all of you and a whole host of other people what He can really do.

Again, thanks to all of you for your prayers, your support and your kindness.

In Christ, John

What I wrote that night sparked something inside of me. I wanted to share this story with the readers of my paper. It was

A Journey of Faith

an undeniable urge, and I realize now it was God using my position in the workplace to further Jacob's story and His kingdom. Before turning in to bed that night, I wrote a column that would be shared with so many people, it still astounds me. It's been used by doctors to help grieving parents who face situations similar to what we were facing. It's been used by pastors to help grieving parishioners. It's made its way to monks in the Bronx, and to a mother in Mississippi who lost her child at birth. How far it has reached I truly will never know because each time I think it has stopped, someone else tells me he or she has read it. What I do know is that every word in there was God's.

"How long is a lifetime?"

The concept of the word "lifetime" has become very new to me in the past week.

If you asked the average person how long a lifetime is, they would tell you, "a long time," or something of the like.

In part, I agree. I remember times when a lifetime seemed like forever. For example, the time between when my mom would say "Wait until your father gets home!" and when he actually got home, that seemed like a lifetime, even if it was only five minutes.

The time between when the line drive came off the bat and when it hit me in the throat on the pitcher's mound, that seemed like a lifetime, even though it was only a split second.

But now, suddenly, a lifetime takes on a whole new definition for me.

There's a good chance that my child, who last week we found out was a boy, will live only a few hours after being born in January. My son, Jacob Alexander Agliata, needs a miracle or he will most likely live his lifetime with his mom and dad in about as long as it takes to drive from here to Indianapolis.

Jacob's Story

I've made that drive numerous times. It's not a long time.

But you know what? It's something.

My wife and I have had now more than two weeks of what most would consider the worst news you could possibly imagine. This tiny person you've grown to love even though you've never actually touched him has a problem that the doctors aren't hopeful they can fix, and even if they could, aren't hopeful that irreversible damage hasn't been done.

We pray for a miracle and have received word of prayer coming from as near as next door and as far away as Japan. But, with tremendous effort and many tears, we are growing to accept the probability that even the most advanced medical science can't help us. Our best hope without God's intervention is that my wife is able to carry Jacob to full term and deliver him without incident; then the doctors will hand him to us for those few hours that he is able to live.

Somewhere along the line, I redefined the terms they were giving us. It wasn't "those few hours" anymore. That's too short. Instead, it is this: We have a lifetime to spend with our son.

No, if all goes as it's been going, it won't be the lifetime that you picture when you think of having a son. There will be no first words. No first steps. No first ballgame or first concert. No first date, first prom, first time away from home, first job, first love, first and only marriage or first grandchild. But it is a lifetime nonetheless.

In that lifetime, we will be able to tell our son everything he means to us, everything he has brought us simply through his coming to be. We'll be able to touch him and hold him, smell him and

78

A Journey of Faith

love him. We'll take in all that this tiny miracle has to offer us and fill him with all the love we have to give him. We'll be able to create memories that will last us the rest of our lifetimes.

A lifetime with our son will most likely not be what the average person thinks of when you ask him how long a lifetime lasts. But, if that's all God is going to grant us, then a lifetime—Jacob's lifetime—is enough to fill our hearts with the love he—and He—is all about.

The response to the column was amazing, humbling me beyond belief. The e-mails and notes I received in the days and weeks following its publication were strengthening. What was most amazing to me was that all of these messages were from people I had never met before. They were strangers, people who simply liked to read the weekly community newspaper. They've all become so much more.

John,

Thanks for being so transparent in your column on Thursday. I cut out the article and put it on the kitchen table where I can pray for you every time I sit down to work or eat. I'm praying for you now—in public school!

Ruthie

John,

Our church, my family, and I are praying for you, your wife, and your baby. God is in control and loves you dearly.

In Jesus' love, Doug Shope
Pastor, Oxford Church of the Nazarene

Jacob's Story

John,

I feel like I know you. I've read many of your editorials in *The Oxford Press* and I could tell that you were a Christian. I praise you for your boldness in what you say. You're just what we need in Oxford today!

I want you to know that I've just read about your baby and I'm praying this prayer for you:

Dear Lord, you have a plan for each of us and it's not for us to question your plan. Your love will sustain us no matter what you decide for our lives. Please know that much love has already been showered upon this still-developing infant. This child will be nurtured and cared for and brought up to know and love you. Please give your powerful healing touch to this life and give the doctors and nurses all the knowledge and care to do whatever this baby needs. You are the ultimate healer. We place this child in your hands. In Jesus name, I pray. Amen.

Blessings, Trish

Mr. Agliata, I finished your column this afternoon with a tear running down my cheek. I, like you, believe in the power of prayer and will certainly keep you and your wife and baby in mind. I went through a very difficult pregnancy and delivered a 3 1/2 pound preemie (who today is a healthy 7-year-old). I pray not only for a similar happy ending to your story, but for peace and strength as you face this wrenching time.

John,

Words can't convey to you my empathy and compassion. I am one of those parents who will come crawling out of

A Journey of Faith

the woodwork—another parent who faced such gut-wrenching, soul-zapping news. My husband calls us—you, your wife, us—The Club.

Our son was born 16 weeks early at 1-1/2 pounds. His APGARs (the test right after birth for breathing, skin color, heart rate...where a typical infant should score a 9 or 10) were -0- for the 1st minute, -1- after 3 minutes and a whopping -3- after 5 minutes. The MD came out to the waiting room and told my husband, "You had a son." Had? Have? Without betraying his most personal pleadings and prayers and demands, let me say your words hit home...way home...with both of us. We were given a 30 percent chance AT BEST that night for Kyle to survive. One more hour...please God. After 88 days in the NICU and 37 chest x-rays and multiple infections and 3 EEGs and 3 EKGs and 6 blood transfusions and coming home on oxygen and post-NICU surgery, Kyle is now 21 months, 25 pounds, running around getting into every "no-no" and babbling a blue streak. Our primary nurse calls him the first true miracle in her career. A miracle. There are miracles all around us. I will try not to resort to trite or cliché advice. But please drink in the love and positive thoughts and prayers and healing energy that surrounds you—from all of us in The Club and all of the other caring people around you. It is powerful. Scott, Kyle and I are praying for you, your wife and Jacob Alexander.

Most sincerely, Tammi

John,

I am Tammi husband, Scott. Tammi forwarded the correspondence between the two of you and I wanted to reply to your question, and offer my support and prayers as well.

Jacob's Story

We were deeply moved by your article in *The Oxford Press*. I shared many of the same feelings you expressed in your editorial, but was unable to verbalize them as eloquently as you. I remember thinking that "it's been 1 hour...I've been a father for 1 hour." The mixed emotions of fear and dread sometimes took a respite, replaced with feelings of pride—"I am a father—even if it's for an hour, two hours..." only to resurface again and again throughout the night. You are absolutely correct in your editorial. There is so much joy felt in a lifetime—even those that do not fit the conventional definition.

Please know that my deepest good wishes are with you, your wife and your son. Enjoy each precious moment shared. I know you will.

Scott

God brought many angels into our lives through this situation. The piles of e-mails that filled my work account taught me a lot about how to look at life. Being a newspaperman tends to make you jaded. You hear about the dregs of society, people doing horrible things to one another, tragedy, death and despair. You can find good out there, but you really have to search for it, and then you think if it takes that much effort to find, then it must not compare in quantity or strength to the bad that happens every day. These e-mails were showing me that wasn't true. Quickly, I was learning that the good is more vast and much stronger than the bad. It might not seem like it because bad stands up and is seen and draws attention to itself, while good is content to exist outside the limelight. The people who were e-mailing me their support weren't doing it for any selfish reason. They weren't doing it to be seen as good. They were doing it because they simply *are* good. This realization started me off on a life-changing course that altered how I view

A Journey of Faith

daily existence. It's not about the bad that stands up and cries, "Look at me!" It's about the hidden good that fills so many of us, the positive that is just waiting for the right opportunity to come out. This good is not necessarily as bright and noticeable as a blazing sun, but maybe as small as a tiny pinprick of light that illuminates someone's darkest moments.

Chapter Twelve

All in God's Hands

Mothers are full of little sayings that confound their children. One of my mother's favorites was "A watched pot never boils." Now, aside from being totally inaccurate—the pot will, indeed, eventually boil—it was something that I never truly understood when I was young and the words always seemed out of place with the present situation. When I would say that I couldn't wait for Santa to come, I'd get "A watched pot never boils." When I said that I was looking forward to the end of school, I'd get "A watched pot never boils." It got to the point that I associated anything I was really excited about with boiling water.

Now, however, I understand what my mother was talking about. As Monday progressed, we waited anxiously for word from Dr. Polzin on the latest test results. Carla and I tinkered

A Journey of Faith

around the house, and I came up with my own offshoot of my mother's favorite phrase: "A watched phone never rings."

Inside, I understood that Dr. Polzin had other patients, that he was a busy man with more to do in the average day than a newspaperman has to do in the average week. He had other people waiting for him to be their voice of hope. But on the surface I couldn't prevent some selfishness from boiling up. As noon came and went, I tried to stay busy playing computer games, reading, watching television. I also prayed.

"God, please give us some hope today. Please don't close all the doors. So many people are asking for you to heal Jacob. Don't you hear them? Don't you hear me? No matter what, Lord, you've got me. But think about how glorious it would be to have me take Jacob around to different places and when his story comes up I'll tell them about how it can only be attributed to You, God, that he's here today, that the doctors thought there wasn't a chance but You thought otherwise. Wouldn't that be great for Your glory, God?"

The different things that Dr. Polzin could say swirled through my head. First, the urine tests could be fine and our nightmare would be over. God's miracle would be real. Second, the urine tests could reveal that things were at a level in which they would do surgery on Jacob inside Carla's womb to put a shunt in him that would bypass the blockage and return the amniotic fluid levels to normal. This would be done only if the tests showed the kidneys were functioning at a level that would enable him to live once he was born. Otherwise, it would be a wasted procedure for Jacob and a risky one for Carla. Or third, the urine test would reveal that kidney function remained at levels that were incompatible with life.

Around 3 p.m., the phone finally rang. I jumped on it before the first ring could begin to fade. Dr. Polzin's familiar voice asked to speak with Carla. As she got on the line, I stayed on the phone to hear what was being said.

Two hours later, I wrote this update to the e-mail list:

85

Jacob's Story

Hi all.

Well, we got the news that we pretty much expected from the doctor today. The tests on the urine drawn from Jacob's bladder on Friday showed that kidney function is not at a level that would support life. It also isn't at a level that would lead them to do a shunt because it would have no effect...the kidneys still wouldn't work upon birth.

The good news is that the lungs have developed well and are strong. This is good because it means that we could possibly have as long as a week with Jacob after he is born. It's amazing how "good news" has been redefined in the span of about two weeks.

So here's what we are facing now for the near future. They will continue to do infusions of fluid for a few more weeks to aid the lung development. This is to help us reach our goal of spending time with our son in our arms. After 23 weeks, the fluid isn't necessary anymore to aid lung development, so we most likely will stop doing the infusion at that point because it increases the risk of miscarriage with each needle stick through Carla into the placenta. We will continue to be monitored closely by the doctors for a variety of things. The biggest is to make sure the heart is still beating. Without the fluid in there, there is an increased risk of the baby pulling the umbilical cord and detaching it from the placenta. If this happens, his heart will eventually stop and Carla will be induced to deliver our stillborn little one.

Let me sum it all up by saying this: We have gone the medical route. They've done everything they can do to try to find us a cure. There will be no cure from the medical establishments. We are out of options. We've explored every avenue there is to take.

A Journey of Faith

So now, if our baby is to have a long life, it's all in God's hands. We still believe a miracle could happen. Some of you have shared your miracle stories—some of which have happened to you, some to people you know. Those stories strengthen us to believe that, yes, something like that could happen to us. I ask all of you...don't stop praying for that miracle for us. Yes, we need your prayers for strength, but we ask that you don't stop praying for that miracle.

Carla and I were talking today and we realized that, through all of you, there are at least 400 or 500 people and as many as 1,000 or more who have said a prayer for us or are continually praying for us. I want you all to stop and think about that. In less than two weeks, look at how many people have been led to talk to God. Through the three of us, hundreds of people, many of whom don't know each other, have united for one cause before God. That's amazing to me and humbles me. It also encourages me.

Carla and I are doing OK. We're holding up well and are strong in our faith. We are both resolute in the fact that we do indeed have a lifetime to spend with our son...his lifetime.

Thank you all for your support, your prayers and your kindness (and for the food some of you have brought!). We continue to thrive off all your support.

Love, John

The responses were almost instantaneous. What touched us so deeply was that not only were they uplifting, they were also insightful.

From our former church pastor and friend who had recently accepted a call to lead a church in Washington state:

Jacob's Story

Dear John and Carla and Jacob,

I cannot express our concerns and care for you three at this time. In contrast John has been so articulate in expressing your anguish and your faithful struggle with God in this situation. I affirm your perspectives and outlook. No one would ever choose the path that you all are on, nor would one who loves you choose it for you, but here you are. In the midst of a fallen broken world things do go wrong. Often God protects us from the manifold dangers of that fallen world, but sometimes He doesn't. And as you have said so well, in the midst of those times we can both cry out for miracles AND be sustained by His comfort and presence in the midst of the brokenness. I am reading Chuck Colson's book *How Now Shall We Live* and in it he says "One of the many great paradoxical truths of the Christian life is that the greatest adversity often produces the greatest blessings." At this point I am sure that you see little blessing in the midst of your pain. The blessing you want most is to see a healthy little boy grow up. But you know that you have seen the blessing of the tenderness and care you have for each other; the blessing of many family and friends who are reaching out in prayer; and the blessing of the reassurances of God's care that come in those surprising ways, sometimes in the middle of a sleepless night. I suggest to you that your raw, honest grappling with this in your lives, and your steadfast faith in a loving God in the face of an apparently unloving situation has been a blessing to many. I believe Jacob is being used by God in his own special way. We will continue to cry with you, hope with you and pray with you.

Love, Wayne and Ruth

Cheryl McKee, a church friend who would go on to play such an important role in Jacob's birth, wrote the following:

88

A Journey of Faith

Yes, we will continue to pray as will all the individuals we have forwarded this to. Someone asked me today how Carla was doing and I said that she was doing well with the prayer support and the love that John has for her courage at this time. I cannot help but think that every nudge and flutter that Jacob is communicating to CARLA is even more special!!!! Yes, weeks seem like a short life span but so precious at the same time.

Miracles are in order and we know who is the best... God!!!! He is good....

Love you guys.... Know that at council tomorrow, you are our focus....

And on top of that, Jacob's story continued to spread. In this case, it was from my college friend Beth to her Aunt Betsy, whom I had never met and now, in this message, to one of Betsy's friends.

Hi! You do not know me, a good friend Betsy has asked for prayer for your family, and I am praying. I am a NICU nurse, and a memory keeper. It is very important to document your event with photographs, so that later you and your wife will have a record of this life-changing event. Hopefully, the nurses will encourage photographs, cuddling and time spent with Jacob, no matter how God chooses to unfold the events of Jacob's life. This memory book will serve as a witness of the grand miracle, if a healing is to take place, or could serve as a tool for healing if God chooses to take Jacob home. It can serve as a tool for both of you to express your emotions and feelings.

If I can be of any help, please contact me. I will be lifting up your family in prayer.

Warmly, Lynne in FL

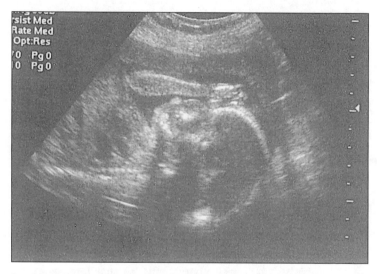

Jacob's ultrasound picture, hand resting on his forehead.

Chapter Thirteen

Lifting up the Troubled Spirit

From there, life became a series of doctor's appointments. As I wrote in the update message, our hope was no longer in the medical route. The frequent Level II ultrasounds were not something we believed would show us that things had medically changed. Rather, they became something much more important: They were time with our son.

It was odd at first, but I started looking forward to these ultrasounds. I could see our little Jacob clearly, and we would ask Dr. Polzin to hold the receiver still so we could watch him move. We also requested that he print out as many pictures as possible. The cutest thing was that Jacob's right arm was positioned so his hand rested on his forehead in a sort of "woe is me" pose. As he grew and Carla's belly swelled, he would spend literally hours rhythmically tapping on Carla's belly, sometimes softly,

Jacob's Story

sometimes with enough force to knock my head off of her tummy when we were lounging on the couch at night. To us, the ultrasounds were when we could be parents. We would talk to him, fawn over how cute he looked and stare in amazement at how he moved. We knew we would probably not get a chance to stand by our sleeping child in his crib with awe at the creation God made through us, so we would do it here and now.

There were glimmers of hope throughout the journey that things might not be as they seemed. Jacob simply was anything but a typical case, giving the doctors reason to pause and us enough of a reason to think that maybe our son would live. In one sense, it was cruel to have the ups and the downs that came seemingly with each appointment. It got to the point where the latest "good" news left us shaking our heads and smiling as we left the hospital and walked to our car. Equally crushing were the "bad news" appointments that dashed the hope the "good news" appointments had started to build.

On September 29, I wrote:

Hi all. Another day, another update from the doctors.

We went for a level II ultrasound, which is just an ultrasound on steroids, I guess, because it costs a bazillion dollars to make the machine and it sees things other ultrasounds can't. ANYWAY...the ultrasound revealed that Jacob's lungs are normal for his stage of development. That's a good thing. That could mean days instead of hours, if that's God's plan. The kidneys are still larger than they should be and the contents of the urine still isn't good. This means that it is the doctors' best educated guess that, if Carla goes to term and delivers Jacob OK, he will eventually slip into a coma and die, perhaps in two days, perhaps in ten. All in all, they say, it is a very peaceful way to die, with no pain. The good news, if you keep this all in perspective, is that there would be a chance we would be able to take Jacob home with

A Journey of Faith

us. I'll spare you all the details, but if the lungs are OK and there's nothing more they can do to try to "fix" anything, then he would be a normal little boy whose kidneys will eventually fail and that can happen just as well in the nursery his momma and daddy painted for him than in some icky hospital where no one could be of any help anyway. The doctor said that we might be a good candidate for neonatal hospice. I didn't even know there was such a thing.

Of course, the doctor said there is a chance that the little guy could surprise us and pop out of there with better kidney function than expected. They won't rule that out, and even if THEY did, I don't think there's a chance that I could give up hope. I promised Jacob I would NEVER give up hope...not until he takes his last breath and goes to be with God, whether that's at two hours, two days or 200 years.

So, as for Carla and me, we remain strong and do our best. We have weaker moments, to be sure, where the only things we can say is "THIS REALLY SUCKS!" But the prayers of so many still keep coming in, as do letters, cards, e-mails, flowers and even food to help us get through those tough times when cooking is the last thing on our minds.

So I still don't pretend to know truly what God is doing, but I do know that He gave this situation to two people who could, in the long run, handle it. It's not easy, of course. It's the hardest thing we've ever had to face in our lives. But we both are secure in the knowledge that we will make it through whatever is to come...together...and together with God.

Please keep praying. Please pray that we're able to go full term with Jacob and that God would give strength

Jacob's Story

to his kidneys, that we're able to take him home. And again, please pray for each other.

In Christ, John

The prayers that kept coming in from others and the lengths people went to let us know they were praying was astounding. There is something that happens to the troubled spirit when it is uplifted in a single, massive voice. Bad days aren't quite as bad. Good days are just that much better. And overall, life is livable during a time when it most apparently would not be. I found that the care of others opened my heart completely to God for the first time in my life. There was nothing I was holding back. Everything I said or did was done with Him in mind. It was the start of a new way of life for me. I found that when I totally laid myself bare before God, I had such a thirst for Him that it led me to seek Him in ways I never had before. And every time, God met me in my search.

At the same time God was religiously educating me, I was getting an unexpected medical education. Technical terms to describe Jacob's latest development rolled off my tongue like words I learned in first grade. I began to be able to anticipate where Dr. Polzin was going when he explained to us what he saw in Jacob's development on the ultrasound. All these changes, religious and medical, were evident in the updates I wrote to an ever-expanding group of people.

On October 11, I wrote:

Hello all. It's been more than a week, hasn't it? We actually had a whole week last week with no doctor's appointments! Imagine that?

We've had two this week, so let me update you on where things stand. Good news first, as always. The good news is that the lung development continues to look pretty good, which means that the lack of fluid hasn't put pressure on the chest cavity to a point where the chest is putting pressure on the heart. The lungs are good sized, which is encouraging. They're not great, but they're good. The doc said they are at the borderline of normal/abnormal. What it means is that the doc doesn't think the lungs should be a problem when Jacob is born, which is good. More good news: There's still fluid around the baby. Totally unexpected, I think. That means the doc thinks that this blockage is only a partial blockage and some urine is getting out, which is good for Jacob in the sense that he'll have some room to move around. More good news: He's just a bit above average in his measurements for his age (that's my boy!).

Now the not-so-good stuff. The kidneys still look bad and the contents of the urine are still bad. The kidneys are enlarged and cystic, meaning they appear to have these black spots. Bottom line is that, according to everything the doctor sees, the kidneys will not function well enough to support life long-term. They simply are not doing what kidneys should do with waste. And even if we got to the point that we could do a transplant (he'd have to live a year, which is highly unprobable, says the doc), the poor kidney development would have had an effect on other things, like thyroid, adrenal glands, etc., and, according to the doctors, while those things aren't prohibitive, they usually aren't things that can be overcome. More bad things: The good news that the blockage isn't total actually reveals some bad news. The kidneys aren't producing as much urine now, which means that as the baby develops and waste becomes more concentrated the kidneys aren't doing their thing.

So those are the particulars, and it's really nothing new in terms of anything that will change our focus on this whole issue. Jacob is still our son, he's still adorable on

Jacob's Story

the ultrasound, with his little hand resting on his forehead and one of his legs folded under his little butt. The MEDICAL prognosis is still not good, but the Lord has the ultimate say, so we wait on Him to see what's going to happen. We will never give up hope as long as Jacob's heart is beating, which it is doing very well and is so comforting for both of us to see on these ultrasounds.

The bottom line is this: We know the road ahead doesn't look good. We know that, without a miracle, Jacob will not live very long at all. But we also know that there has been so much GOOD that has already come from this. So many people have heard about this situation and been touched by it, and I am humbled by that. I got a letter today from a complete stranger who is a reader of the paper I work for. She had been following the columns I have written and basically took our son with her on her trip to Italy. She got the nuns praying for us, she had masses said in Jacob's name, she got a cardinal to pray for Jacob, she had someone who had an audience with the pope take Jacob's name to the pope for prayer. Remember, this was a complete stranger... someone who has never met us. Do you see how amazing that is, how KIND that is? Remember that when you think society is so evil...that people ARE kind beyond your wildest dreams. As this woman wrote, Jacob's "been in our hearts for ten days on this trip, and he has some pretty powerful people in Rome, from the Vatican on down and in the surrounding cities praying for him. It is our hope that he will be your (I originally typed this as 'our' and changed it to 'your' for I guess I feel subconsciously he belongs to all of us) miracle baby, and whatever happens, we know he will be held tightly in God's hands."

She's right...Jacob is all of yours. All of you who have lifted him up in prayer, whether one time or daily, Jacob

A Journey of Faith

is yours because you've petitioned God on his behalf. I am so thankful for that.

How are Carla and I holding up? OK, under the circumstances. I think it can be best said this way: We sometimes get tired. Perhaps weary is a better word because sleep can't solve this kind of fatigue. But that's the body. In spirit, we are strong. As a couple, we are strong. And we are so thankful for our friends, our families and the complete strangers of this world who just simply care.

I can't say it enough: When you get cut off on the highway the next time or your boss is a jerk or someone says something that hurts you, remember that there are many GOOD people and much kindness out there. Sometimes it might be hard to see, but if everyone on this list just starts by getting the ball rolling, going out of their way for someone else, do you see how this could snowball? We would actually be creating a better world instead of just wishing for it.

I've gone on long enough for now, I guess. Sorry if I bored ya'll! I just am so filled with the spirit after getting a letter like the one I got today.

We remain thankful and appreciative of your letters, e-mails, visits and prayers. I don't know where we'd be without them (and the great food you guys have sent our way! We could create a Jacob's Cookbook out of all the good stuff you guys have brought!).

Please continue to pray for Jacob and for strength for us, and please...pray for each other.

In Christ, John

Chapter Fourteen

Joy and Strife

The single most amazing thing that happened while Jacob—and Carla—grew was that for the first time in my life I truly felt God. In the midst of all the worry and doubt over how things would go, I became filled with an indescribable joy, the feeling that I was literally in God's arms, that God was with me wherever I went, in whatever I was doing. It was as real to me as being able to talk to Carla. God was there.

An irony comes with such a feeling, though. It creates friction. There was such a sense of peace in my heart, and such a sense of wonderment that God was so directly involved in ministering to my heart, that I walked around almost giddy with a smile on my face most of the time. At first, I couldn't comprehend why others around me didn't share this joy when I told them about how I could feel God's hand. Many remained

A Journey of Faith

morose, talking about this "horrible" situation and this "tragedy." Inside, it didn't feel horrible, and it didn't feel like a tragedy.

Tiny battles broke out between me and my family, and the emotions of the times fanned the flames of those battles into full-fledged blow-ups. Didn't they get it? How could a situation be so horrible and tragic if God was right there working in it? There was such an assurance in my heart that Jacob's life before it had officially begun had meant something, and God's closeness in the situation told me He wasn't done yet working through him or us. Why didn't my parents, and especially my father, get it?

My father and I at some point late in my high school years realized we were as close as a father and son could get, so much so that when Carla and I got married, he was my best man. But his religious views had become vastly different from mine, not because he'd changed, but because of what I was experiencing with God. He, like some others around me who thought my talk of seeing God right there in the midst of this was crazy, couldn't grasp what I meant when I talked about the joy in the situation. He had never experienced God that way before, and he wasn't exactly open to trying to understand how his son could be smiling in the midst of such a medically challenging situation. To him, his grandson was most likely going to die and there was nothing good about that, regardless of what was happening through Jacob in other people's lives. That wedge between us created the most heartache in me during the entire ordeal with Jacob. My father, my best man, was now seemingly a million miles away from the point where I stood. I questioned God on this: How could you fill me with such a spirit of wonder for You and in doing so allow such a rift to develop between my father and me? The answer only created more of a rift between me and my family.

God calls us to give our primary allegiance to Him. That's ahead of loyalty to country, ahead of loyalty to our spouse and ahead of loyalty to our parents. If ever there's a question of whom you are going to follow, God always wins. In my young adult life,

Jacob's Story

it hadn't been that way. My father was my rock. He guided me in financial decisions, job decisions, personal decisions. It was his advice I would seek before making any major move in my life, although I didn't necessary always take it. Now, I felt I was being called to take my needs to a different Father, and that Father's answers were increasingly different from my dad's. God never promises harmony, but He does promise a heavenly reward for those who follow Him. I came to the realization that these battles were in no way caused by my parents. They hadn't changed. It was I who was changing. Accepting that direction in my life months later gave me peace about the changing nature of my relationships with family, especially my father. Facing the decisions we faced with Jacob, relying on God and realizing He ministered to my heart every time I sought Him made me more of a man and less my father's little boy. It was a change, I realized, that happens in every productive and healthy father-son relationship. Ours just happened in the midst of the hottest fires, which also happen to be needed to mold the best clay.

During all of this, days hit when it seemed like the world was stacked against us. We would search for one hint of good news—even in the altered, limited definition it now took in our lives—from each appointment, but there were times when it was hard to find. Still, God's presence was so real in my life that the joy remained and shined through in the update messages He led me to write.

On October 19, I wrote:

> We met with a neonatologist for a consultation on basically what we can expect. He had reviewed all our information, talked with various other doctors, did his own research, etc. Basically, I wish I could say there's an ounce of good news in this. OK, maybe I can. The good

A Journey of Faith

news is that they cannot be 100 percent certain that Jacob will die soon after he is born.

The bad news is that, in his opinion, there is a reasonable medical certainty that Jacob will die within a few hours or days after being born. His opinion is that the blockage that first tipped us off to the problem happened early on in the pregnancy, when the tissue that would become the kidneys was smaller than a pea. The blockage prevented the kidneys from forming normally, and since the kidneys are done forming in terms of fetal development, how they look now is how they will be, at best. That's not good. What he expects as time goes on is, as the kidneys grow with the baby, the tissue will appear more abnormal with more cysts (black spots where kidney-specific tissue was to have formed). Kidney function, which is hard to detect now, will get worse and when Jacob is born, he will have at most several days until the toxins build up in his body, eventually stopping his heart. The other problem is the lungs. There is a good chance that, though the lungs are at the bottom end of the normal range in size right now, they will start to not look so good as time goes on before he is born, so much so that when he is born his lungs won't be able to support life, at which time, unless we take heroic action, he will stop breathing and die.

That's the medical stuff. Here's my thoughts: I don't know if there's any other way to say this, but to be able to sit there with some sense of comfort and strength and sanity while a doctor tells you all the different ways and specifics in which your son will die...to be able to do that is a testament to the Lord's presence in our lives. Does it hurt? Darn right. And do we cry? Of course. But somehow we sit there and hear about what Jacob's life will be like and how it will end and I still have this overwhelming sense of peace that, even if they are right, he

Jacob's Story

is going to a place that I long to go—a place much better than this, where that spirit of his that keeps him kicking Carla to comfort her and let her know he's OK and still breathing is free of the constraints of his damaged earthly body. According to the doctors, he shouldn't be kicking as much now as he once did because there's not enough fluid and there's not enough room. But he kicks like crazy. This is such a comfort to us because of the doctor's warnings that he could damage the umbilical cord at any time and that would kill him (low-fluid environment would lead to this). So he kicks and kicks so Carla knows... "Hey Mom, I'm OK.... And send down another burrito, will ya?" So many of you have said you feel so strongly he is going to be OK. I wish I could share that optimism. But ya know what, in some sense, he IS going to be OK, free of this damaged body to be with God, the ultimate Father.

We saw where Jacob will be born. We saw the room we hope to be in, surrounded by our close family, if they want to be there when he dies. We met the nurses and told them our wishes, for footprints and pictures and all those other things. And then we left and we cried. For many years, we've had the "Footprints" poem in our various homes. I never thought I'd be living "Footprints." It's an amazing thing to feel as if God is picking you up and carrying you through the tough times. Carla will be the first one to tell you I'm not that strong. I'm not that strong to sit there and listen to all the ways our baby could die. But GOD is that strong. And God gives us comfort. Please pray for us and don't give up praying for that miracle. Now that all the doctor angles are gone, if Jacob survives, no one can deny God's hand. But even if that doesn't happen, no one can deny God's hand in all of you and what you've meant to us.

In Christ, John

Chapter Fifteen

What If?

On a night of goblins and ghouls came evidence of the biggest change in our lives. We sat on the porch as the sun fell, the first hints of cold fall weather in the air. In between dumping candy into the bags of trick-or-treaters, Carla and I found ourselves in a "what-if" conversation. The question came up: What if you could change everything and have Jacob be 100 percent fine and healthy, but you would have to give up all that God has done in your life through this and also all the good that God has done in others' lives through this? Would you?

The answer was obvious, wasn't it? I mean, surely we would take our healthy, happy son and run, right? My mind wandered to some of the messages we'd gotten since August 30th in response to e-mails and newspaper columns that spoke to what Jacob was doing in people's lives.

Jacob's Story

From the sister of my college friend, Beth:

John & Carla,

Yes, let's keep bombarding God with prayers [that made me laugh]. And it's nice to hear that there are so many good people in this country. Sometimes I wonder if it was selfish for us to have our son. After all, what kind of world will he inherit? Your story is inspiring to us! Thank you for the words of encouragement about society. Sometimes I get so bogged down in the crappy stuff in the news.

From my friend, Ted:

I just want say you've been a real inspiration to me how you're handling this pregnancy. You've kept your faith, which is so difficult in trying times, and you're staying positive. I don't know when or how, but I know you will be rewarded. But it is so great to see how you handle things.

From Ted's wife, Monica:

I had a thought today about Jacob. How many parents can brag on their son the way you and Carla can? I mean, really? How many people can honestly brag about the number of souls your son has won over to the Lord in his lifetime? Granted, he has a bit of a head start. I'm sure you have yet to comprehend the magnitude. Awards, trophies, honors, etc. cannot measure up to the accomplishments of master Jacob Alexander. Be proud of your son and his ministry. Learn from it as you begin your path of evangelism. He has truly been a gift.

A Journey of Faith

From a friend of my parents, Kathleen:

Dear John and Carla,

I guess you know how much you and Jacob are a part of my every day. I get teary-eyed in the strangest places. I wish the news were more encouraging, but, as you said—it will be God's will for whatever reason He has. Maybe it is to remind us all that there is incredible good in what sometimes seems to be a very cruel world.

From my friend, Jen:

John,

I cried when I read your message yesterday, and I'm still fighting back tears now. I was thinking yesterday that maybe the actual meaning of the "great commission" or the main real challenge to Christians is to be encouraging to each other even when we're scared too. I'm so scared about Jacob. I picture him looking like my nephew James, and I bet he will sort of look like him because James looks a little like Carla and he had reddish hair when he was born. I find myself playing that game with God where I try to bargain with Him, and try to trade my life or behaviors or future for Jacob's health. To the logical world, I'm sure this is ridiculous—I haven't seen you in years, and I barely knew you then. I've never even met Carla, and I'm not related to you guys...why should I be SO emotionally involved?

Is the brotherhood of life in Christ the answer? That would explain why I feel like Jacob is my nephew and you are my brother. That would explain why my sister and her husband also cry over Jacob, when they've never even talked to you. I hope you're all right, but you are so strong that it amazes me. God does crazy things and

Jacob's Story

likes to trick us with His timing, I think—like with Abraham and Isaac, or with my dad when he had his heart attack, or like when my sister almost died having James. He likes to save us at the very last minute. Also, as my brother was pointing out in church this weekend, throughout the Bible God has shown that He is moved by the prayers of His people, and that He has mercy on us when we want something very much.

I love you.

From Emilie, the wife of *The Oxford Press* editor, Bob, whose entire family—21-year-old daughter Meggan, 19-year-old son Christian and 14-year-old daughter Elise—has become good friends,

The growing number of people I send your messages to, thank me for sending them. They are blessed by your faith, your story and the need for them to pray. Keep the messages going out! Elise is crazy about you two. It is a strong witness to her to follow your faith journey during this time in your lives. I hope she carries it with her forever as her faith continues to be challenged and the doubts mount. Did I tell you about my friend from Anchorage, Alaska, who used to work with homeless people? She is blown away by your faith, courage and willingness to witness to so many people. This is bigger than all of us. No matter what happens, Jacob has already made a difference in many lives—more difference than many people make in years.

Love you, Emilie

From Pastor Larry, who would play such an important role in Jacob's life and in our lives during and after,

A Journey of Faith

The testimony of his life and the awesome faith you and Carla have shown has without question drawn many closer to the Lord. I also feel many have received Christ as their personal Lord as they have known what Christ has done in your lives. Our Lord has spoken to many through the quiet voice of Jacob as well as through the written word you have shared with many. And, Carla's smile has been a testimony in many ways. I shared her smile, your words and Jacob's life last Thursday at a church service I conducted at Westover.

They were blessed and rejoiced in your faith and trust in our Lord.

Thinking about those things, how should we answer the question? Would we give everything up for all these people and the others that would be touched in the months ahead, not to mention the work God was doing in our own lives, to heal Jacob.

I wrote this e-mail update several days later:

Hi all. I hope you are all well and enjoying the fall weather. There's nothing new medically to report. We have a few appointments this week, however, including an ultrasound on Thursday that will tell us how Jacob's lungs are doing. I wish I could tell you I feel this great sense of optimism. I don't. But I also don't feel overwhelmingly sad about that. Of course it hurts and of course I am sad to a degree, but not as most would expect. Carla and I sat on our porch Halloween night handing out candy to all the little ones. A little aside...was it just us or did you notice that everything had to be "dead" this year. When I was young, we dressed up as ballplayers, businessmen, cheerleaders and princesses. We saw so many people dressed like that, but DEAD. A ballplayer with a ball smashed into her hat and

107

Jacob's Story

blood all over her face. A dead cheerleader. A bludgeoned princess. It made us look forward to the good old-fashioned UNdead like Dracula. Ha.

Anyway, sorry for the digression. We were talking in between handing out candy and we approached a subject nervously, both afraid, I think, of the other taking it the wrong way. The gist of it, though, was that, even in this time where everything seems so HORRIBLE, we feel...joyous. Joyous? Joyous?!?!? How could THAT be? A friend helped Carla realize it. It's because we feel we're walking so closely with God. I have never felt this close to God. Which raises the question: Would you give up that closeness with God...that feeling that you at times are actually lifted up by His love and comforted, that he is WITH you so closely, to make everything OK with Jacob??? What a hard question. Of course my ideal would be to have this feeling and have everything be FINE with Jacob. That's my ideal. But that's not reality. The fact is, it is solely through God's love for His people that we are able to be joyous much of the time these days. More joyous in God's love than EVER before. The bottom line answer to the question is "I don't know." I would love Jacob to be OK. But I would not want to lose this closeness with God for anything. Selfish human desire tells me to trade anything for Jacob's health, but there's so much more to living life than selfish human desires. Is it barbaric and horrible, then, to say, no, I wouldn't trade Jacob's health to go against God?

Well, all, I'll be in touch after our Thursday appointment, I'm sure. Please pray for us and for Jacob and for complete healing. And please, pray for each other.

In Christ, John

Chapter Sixteen

Reality

If dealing with the constant discouraging news from doctors was challenging, preparing for other potential realities bordered on cruel. On a crisp fall morning I found myself with my father in a cemetery finding a final resting place for Jacob should he die. I stood at the foot of a huge cross bearing the image of Jesus. My hands were jammed in my pocket and my head was down, tears falling down my face. This had become my reality. At 26 years old, I had to prepare to bury my son.

I didn't want to be in that cemetery. I didn't want to face the reality that the doctor's best prognosis gave us just days to spend with our boy. Yet, I had to. I had to because the doctors had also told us there was an increased risk Carla would deliver early, and reality forced me to face that I did not want my son

Jacob's Story

discarded like medical waste. That reality forced me to face cemeteries and talks of caskets and funeral services for Jacob.

The reality was harsh, but the spot was beautiful, all things considered. It was in a section of St. Stephen's Cemetery in Hamilton, Ohio, reserved just for babies. As my father talked to a groundskeeper ten feet away, I looked at the names on the gravestones marking the final resting place for the broken bodies of babies who had died too soon. It stopped me in my tracks.

I became a journalist out of necessity. It wasn't my initial plan. My initial plan was to pitch for the New York Yankees, but a serious elbow injury ended even the most remote part of that dream. With that dream gone, I looked for something new, and in that search I found journalism. It was the storytelling that got me so intrigued, sitting down with someone to interview them and then turning their life into a story for all to read. Now, in front of me, were the names of 13 babies whose stories I didn't know. In the time since that first cemetery visit, I've learned that the stories of one's life are not limited by the years, months, days or hours one lives. Many great things can be accomplished in a short period of time that speak to the true meaning of life. So what were these babies' stories?

One gravestone has three names on it, Katie, Kelly and Kathy Hileman, who lived and died on July 3, 1990. Next to that was their sister's grave, Andrea Marie Hileman, who died less than a year later.

Michael Edward Truster, who lived and died Dec. 24, 1990, has a gravestone that reads "I pray the Lord my soul to keep" with an etched picture of a little angel. What was the story of this Christmas baby?

Jessica Blakely lived and died March 15, 1991, and as the gravestone reads, was "Here briefly, but in our hearts forever."

Stephanie Ann Puma has a simple gravestone with her name and the date of her life, Nov. 28, 1991.

Kevin Michael Smith, whose gravestone says he was a "beloved son and brother," lived four days in August 1992.

A Journey of Faith

Jennifer Whitely Wilson had two beautiful windmills by her gravestone that day, spinning in the nippy fall breeze. She lived from August 22 through Nov. 10, 1992. "God bless our baby," her gravestone reads.

Kyle Weisenberg lived and died Aug. 20, 1993.

Aaron David Norwick lived and died Nov. 9, 1998. His gravestone reads "In our hearts forever."

Amber Nicole and Nicholas Christopher Gambrell, twins who lived and died July 11, 1999, have a gravestone that reads, "Together forever."

Stephanie Elizabeth LeVan was born Nov. 8, 1999, and died on Dec. 14 of that same year. An etching of her tiny face adorned her gravestone. As I looked at her gravestone I realized that if things went as the doctors thought they would, the body of our son, Jacob Alexander Agliata, would eternally rest next to hers. The thought brought me to tears, and soon I felt my father's arms around me. This would be tough.

Equally tough was the thought of going through childbirth classes with a whole bunch of parents expecting healthy babies who they would raise for years and years. It wasn't that we resented them for their happiness. In fact, God helped us both develop such an intense happiness for parents having normal pregnancies that our joy for them could not be contained. Rather, it was just a form of protecting our hearts. We were committed to walking the path that was in front of us. We'd go through the valley and we'd do God's will. But there were little steps we would take to help us ease the road.

For example, I hadn't been sleeping well for about two months. I could get to sleep OK, and it wasn't that I would have long periods of waking in which I would have to go watch television or read a book. But I wasn't sleeping deeply, tossing and turning and waking in the morning feeling as if I'd been hiking all night instead of resting. So to ease the road, I obtained a prescription sleep aid to help me rest and gather my strength.

Jacob's Story

But for childbirth classes, there didn't seem to be an apparent easy next step like the pills that helped me sleep. Carla didn't want to head into labor not knowing what to expect, but she was hesitant to think she could emotionally stand up to a prolonged childbirth class. I prayed for a solution, and God handed us another angel.

It came in the form of a business-sized envelope left on my desk at work while I was in a meeting. Inside was a letter from a woman named Debbie Anderson, who was a registered nurse and had conducted childbirth classes in the past. Her note was one of support and encouragement and contained lists of support groups and resources to help us along the way. She didn't know at the time that God had planned for *her* to be a key support and resource.

Her note read:

Dear John,

I have read your column weekly since you came to *The Oxford Press*. I have enjoyed your candor and insights. While I was happy for you at the news of a baby-on-the-way (I'm a mom and former childbirth instructor), I was deeply touched by the sad news that followed.

I stopped by the office Friday but you were not there. So I decided to write this note instead.

Until last year, I worked as an obstetrical nurse for McCullough-Hyde Memorial Hospital. Over the 11 years I was there, I took a special interest in supporting families experiencing pregnancy loss. Out of this interest, I developed the enclosed materials: a pamphlet (directed toward staff training) and a booklet (directed toward grieving families). If these would be helpful, please read them. If you already have the support you desire, fine. But if the two of you would like to talk to someone, feel free to call me and set up a time and place.

A Journey of Faith

Know that your family—all three—are in prayers. I'm so very sorry that you are having to face this difficult, heart-wrenching situation.

Sincerely, Debbie Anderson

Debbie was God's answer to our prayers. One phone call later and she agreed to come to our house and do a one-night crash course in childbirth.

When the night came, I was nervous. A complete stranger would be in our house having my wife bent in all sorts of interesting positions and breathing like a deranged asthma patient. That was what I told others when I explained my nerves. The real reason was I didn't know if I could keep it together emotionally.

Debbie arrived at our door with a smile and a handshake. For the better part of four hours, we looked at diagrams, watched videos, asked questions and practiced breathing techniques. I got my ten-count down perfectly, and Carla found a strong affinity for the deep, cleansing breaths that put her in a trance-like state of relaxation. Before Debbie left, we prayed together and cried together. Gone were the nerves of the early evening. She was like part of the family. Jacob was now a part of her, too. When she left, the formal handshakes that we shared when she came transformed into hugs of friendship and connection. We still thank God for the angel He sent us in Debbie.

Chapter Seventeen

Who Am I?

As the nasty weather of the pending Ohio winter hit, we continued to be supported daily by the loving hand of God and the e-mails from our expanded group of prayer warrior friends. Still, something deep inside me was troubled. The messages from people who said they admired our strength, people who said they couldn't handle what we were faced with if they had to walk in our shoes, made me feel as if I was coming across as something I wasn't.

When people said I was strong, I laughed. I wondered what they would think if they caught me in my weak moments, sitting on the floor in Jacob's nursery, crying in the darkness. What if they saw that? What if they saw me on the days I drove home from work, torturing myself with Mark Schultz's "He's My Son" on my car stereo? The thing I value most in people I come in contact with is realism. That's what attracted me so

A Journey of Faith

much to Carla when I met her, a genuine, honest person with no pretense. How real was I being to the people on my e-mail list?

On December 16, the weight of this issue became too much for my soul to bear. I wrote:

> Hi all. There's nothing new medically to update you on, but I just felt led to write this, so I'm going to.
>
> I've been torn on how to say this because I want to make sure it comes out the right way, and it's real tough to get some things across correctly by e-mail. What I want to get across is something I feel is very important, though, so I hope you can understand what I mean in what I write. So many of you have written to us or told us how you admire our strength in this situation we're facing. It amazes me this strength that we talk about, because I know it doesn't come from me. Why? Because I simply know I'm not that strong. I have a history of really retreating when things get tough. In those times, the thought of carrying on a message list like this would have been unthinkable. But God has a plan in all of this, and I'm honored to be His instrument.
>
> The problem I have is that I want to make sure there's an element of realism in what that strength is all about. I think the problem comes from a commonly held belief that a good Christian is a happy Christian. After all, we're told to be thankful in all things, aren't we? I think that some people can see sadness in a Christian as a weakness of faith. The thought shared by these Christians is "What do we have to be sad about? We have JESUS!!!!"
>
> How very true, but how very missing the point. We have Jesus and that is why we should not be overwhelmingly sad about anything. But I look at the Bible and I see those who truly had Jesus, meaning He walked among them, and they showed some very real, very bare emotion. In that, I take comfort in how life really is for Carla and me.

115

Jacob's Story

Because, yes, we are strong and set to do the right thing here for God, but, my God, how hard it is! I sit on the couch with Carla by my side and we're joking around and playing with Jacob by feeling where he kicks and sort of pushing back and I think to myself "Dear GOD...my son is in there and there's something so very wrong with his health" and in an instant I am sad. I am angry. I am scared. In short, I am NOT strong. When I was telling this to someone in our church, she said, "Oh, you mean you're human?" And we laughed because it's so true. We're human and our strength is in our faith but our weaknesses are so glaringly apparent in our day-to-day lives. The sadness that we sometimes DON'T overcome and sometimes go to bed with. The anger that sometimes I CAN'T put some place productive so that it keeps me awake at night. The fear that cripples me so that I can't make a decision on what to drink with dinner, let alone comprehend how I'm going to make a decision when a doctor asks me "Do you want to do X or do you want to do Y?"

My point in telling you all of these things is to say that I believe it is healthy as a Christian to live your real emotions and don't deny them in the name of being a *good* Christian. I believe we should follow biblical examples and not hide from our emotions during times of trial. Peter was anguished at the reality of his denial of Jesus. Jesus himself wept. So I guess what I'm saying is a two-part thing. First, I don't want you to think that Carla and I aren't facing the reality that is before us. The emotions are there, and sometimes they are more than we can handle at any given moment.

Second, and more importantly, I want to encourage you NOT to fall into the trap of what some believe a *good* Christian is. Don't hide from real emotions in times of trial because some believe a *good* Christian is a happy Christian who smiles and keeps his chin up while his

116

A Journey of Faith

world collapses. That's not realistic and it is harmful in the long run. And resist the urge to tell those who are facing trial to be thankful in all things, etc., because that is cheating them of the very real emotions they MUST face before the sun really does shine again.

What, then, can we do as Christians? Don't be afraid to get right down there with the person who is hurting and hurt with them. Walk that walk with them. Cry with them. Be angry with them. Be scared with them. And then walk with them again into the sunshine, whenever that occurs. (And rest assured, it WILL occur if we avail ourselves to God.)

We have been so amazed at the people who want to be down at the hospital when Jacob is born. So many people have done what I just wrote, gotten down into the land of real emotion with us and walked with us. They now feel as though Jacob is part of them, so it's only natural that they'd want to be there to see him. I pray that you all get that chance. Listen. I never expected to be in this position. I was a guy who was filled with so many doubts about God and religion and what it all means. To a large extent, I still am. The questions I had are still there. What does God really want in baptism? Would God really make a whole bunch of people who have no chance at heaven if Jesus is the only way? Does the bread REPRESENT the body of Christ or IS it the body of Christ? Ya know what? I have no clue. I probably never will. And I no longer care. What I do know, and what I do care about, is that God is real because I have felt as though I am in the very palm of His hand throughout all of this, comforted and uplifted and strengthened. So when I feel God saying "write," I'll write, even if I feel the outcome is a bit confusing and incoherent.

I hope you are all well and enjoying the holiday season.

In Christ, John

Chapter Eighteen

Time

With just more than a week to go before Christmas, I began to feel sick. It was nothing entirely unexpected; it seems that every Christmas for the past decade I've been sick to some degree or another. This one, though, was hitting hard. I began to run a fever on Monday night, December 18th, and suddenly I felt like I was burning up and freezing at the same time. I shivered while I sweated beneath two blankets while my eyes refused to focus on the television in front of the recliner in my den. Carla doled out the Tylenol every four hours to take the edge off, but I realized I was going to be in for a pretty miserable next few days.

That night, Carla and I slept in separate rooms for the first time since we found out about Jacob's problem. After getting me settled and sufficiently covered, she went into the guest bedroom and sanitized herself from my germs. It was a horrible night. I tried to fool myself that it was just the sickness weighing on my mind, but I was filled with such a terrible sense that Jacob's time was coming and I wasn't going to be healthy. Without Carla and Jacob by my side in the bed, I felt lost. I didn't realize it until that night, but I had grown so accustomed to being able to reach over and put my hand on Carla's belly, as I had done the first night after we'd learned something was wrong. It was my way of connecting with Jacob, comforting him, or perhaps just comforting myself that he was real and he was right there. Now, with him in another room, that connection was lost.

Sleep was fitful that night as the fever boiled. By morning, it was above 100 degrees, rare for me, since even at my sickest I have rarely run a fever. When I combed my hair after taking a shower, I also notice some painful bumps behind my right ear, swollen lymph nodes, I imagined. This was going to be a Christmas to remember.

Carla awoke before I left for work. She had what was now a weekly appointment that day with Dr. Bonar. Thanks to the fever, for the first time, I wouldn't be going with her to the appointment for fear of infecting other pregnant mothers.

"Are you sure you're going to be OK?" I asked. Together, we were able to face the roomful of pregnant mothers carrying healthy babies with grace and a smile, genuinely happy for their good fortune. Apart, I was unsure of how Carla would react.

"Yes, I'll be fine. It's just a quick appointment," she said. "I'll call you when I get home."

By noon that day, I was shot. Feverish and achy, I left work early and came home to a quiet house. I collapsed into my recliner and was fast asleep when the sound of the rising garage door jolted me awake. The sounds announcing Carla's arrival home had become routine to me in the few short months we'd been living in our new home. It started with the low churning

Jacob's Story

of the automatic garage door lifting. Next came the tinkling of the tags on the dog's collar as he arose from wherever he had crashed and rushed to beat Carla to the door. Then came the rumbling of Carla's car engine as she pulled into the garage. Pause, then the slam of the car door. Finally, the creak of the door opening combined with more tinkling from the dog's collar and my wife's voice yelling, "Down! Good boy!"

Everything went as usual until the end. This time, there was no "Down! Good boy!" There was silence. A few seconds later, the tinkling sound came my way and the dog pranced into the den, his ears slicked back as I've seen him do in only two situations: one, when he's just been yelled at, or two, when Carla's upset. A few seconds later, Carla came in and plopped into the computer desk chair across from me.

"I'm two centimeters dilated and 60 percent effaced," she said, matter-of-factly.

My heart skipped a beat. Dilated? Effaced? Such horribly sterile medical words that I'd only recently come to truly understand through Debbie's childbirth crash course, but now they had such bigger meaning. But what exactly was that meaning? Carla seemed to read my mind.

"That means it could be any time now," she said. "That's what Dr. Bonar said, anyway. It could be today. It could be three weeks from now."

That wasn't the end of it either.

"I've been having contractions all day," she continued. "Nothing major, but it's like it gets real tight for awhile and then lets go. It feels like cramps. Dr. Bonar said they could last until Jacob comes."

There was so much I wanted to say, but I was so tired, so weak, that I only managed a nod.

The rest of the day passed in a blur. I slept, sweated and shivered while Carla tried to keep herself busy with little things around the house. She fixed dinner, but neither of us ate much. I was feeling too ill, and Carla said she felt sick to her stomach.

A Journey of Faith

"I hope I didn't get you sick," I said while we sat with half-eaten platefuls of food in front of us.

"No, I just feel stuffed and crampy."

I retreated back to my den and awaited an ESPN special highlighting a speech by Jimmy Valvano, the former North Carolina State University basketball coach who died of cancer in April 1993. In February, his body ravaged by disease, Valvano had taken the stage at the sports station's annual ESPY awards and given a memorable, emotional acceptance speech for the Arthur Ashe Courage Award. Earlier that day, Valvano had hardly been able to walk. Yet, when the time came, he wouldn't be kept away. The speech had brought tears to my eyes the first time I heard it. Its most memorable line, "Don't give up. Don't ever give up," has been played time and again, but the speech had so much more. Though ill, I was looking forward to watching the speech. Just as it started, though, Carla came into the den. She looked pale, scared.

"I think I might be in labor. The contractions are starting to hurt," she said softly.

"God, no," I prayed silently. "Not now. Please. I'm so ill. What good can I possibly be to her when I am this sick?" The last time I took my temperature, it was approaching 102 degrees.

"Are you sure they're contractions?" I said, realizing immediately how much I sounded like the typical idiotic male. "I mean, do you think it could just be some cramping from the exam?"

"I don't know," she said, and in her voice I could hear fright and uncertainty. "They're lasting about the same amount of time, but they aren't the same distance apart."

We did what many other first-time expecting parents would do: We consulted a textbook a friend had given us on pregnancy. We quickly found the section on false labor, but it proved to be little help. There was nothing there that definitively told us one way or another whether this was real or not.

Jacob's Story

I tried to stay calm, but inside, I was frantic. How would I even be able to get her to the hospital, let alone support her, when I felt like I was going to pass out? "Well, let's get a watch and time them." Carla left and came back quickly with my watch. It wasn't a stopwatch, but it would do. When the next pain hit, I started timing. With my eyes fixed on the sweeping second hand and Carla focused on the pain, the room was silent except for Jimmy Valvano speaking to us from the past, from a time just after Carla and I had started dating

"To me, there are three things we all should do every day," he said. "We should do this every day of our lives. Number one is laugh. You should laugh every day. Number two is think. You should spend some time in thought. Number three is, you should have your emotions moved to tears, could be happiness or joy. But think about it. If you laugh, you think and you cry, that's a full day. That's a heck of a day. You do that seven days a week, you're going to have something special."

The first contractions were seven minutes apart.

"Um, honey. If it's seven minutes, we're in trouble," I said with a smile.

"I know, but the last one was like 20 minutes apart," she said. So we waited and timed the next one. While we did, Jimmy V. kept speaking.

"It's so important to know where you are. I know where I am right now. How do you go from where you are to where you want to be? I think you have to have an enthusiasm for life. You have to have a dream, a goal. You have to be willing to work for it."

These contractions were more than 14 minutes apart.

"Do you think we should call the doctor?" I asked.

"Let's time another one."

Again, I watched the sweeping second hand fly around my watch as the speech continued.

"I just got one last thing, I urge all of you, all of you, to enjoy your life, the precious moments you have. To spend each

A Journey of Faith

day with some laughter and some thought, to get your emotions going. To be enthusiastic every day as Ralph Waldo Emerson said, 'Nothing great could be accomplished without enthusiasm,' to keep your dreams alive in spite of whatever problems you have. The ability to be able to work hard for your dreams to come true, to become a reality."

This contraction was only three-and-a-half minutes apart.

"What?!" I said, wide-eyed.

"Time another one," Carla said.

Jimmy V. continued: "I know I gotta go, I gotta go, and I got one last thing and I've said it before and I want to say it again. Cancer can take away all my physical abilities. It cannot touch my mind, it cannot touch my heart and it cannot touch my soul. And those three things are going to carry on forever. I thank you and God bless you all."

This time, they were eight minutes apart. I looked at the clock. It was 9:15 p.m. "Let's call the doctor," I said.

As Carla dialed, I thought about what had just happened, how what most likely was the beginning of Jacob's arrival had played out while the inspirational words of Jimmy Valvano played in the background. As corny as it might sound, it had inspired me. If that man could get up on stage in front of thousands in the audience and millions watching on television, his body ravaged by cancer, and be so brave, I sure as heck could be brave with a little fever and same aches and chills. If it was time to go, I was ready to go. Somehow, it would be OK because there was simply no other choice.

Carla returned from the kitchen. "The doctor said to sit tight. He said to take a bath to relax and try to get some sleep. If I can sleep through the contractions, he said, it's not real labor because labor pains would keep me awake."

"Well, OK then," I said with a smile. I got up and went into the bathroom and began running the water for Carla's bath. "Just try to relax. Maybe this is all nothing. Maybe you're just worried because Dr. Bonar said you were partially dilated."

123

Jacob's Story

"Yeah, maybe," she said. She didn't sound convinced. Frankly, I don't think I'd been that convincing because I wasn't convinced myself.

By the time Carla got done with her bath, I had fallen into a fitful sleep on the bed. For the second night in a row, we slept apart. And if I thought last night had been bad, this night was a thousand times worse. Sleep came in ten minute increments as I strained to listen down the hall to the guest bedroom where Carla had gone. I could hear the dog pacing back and forth, the telltale tinkling of his tags. I could hear the cuckoo clock downstairs every half-hour. And I could hear the bed squeak every once in awhile, as if Carla were trying to get comfortable. One thing I wasn't hearing was silence. Silence that would have meant sleep.

At just after 1:45 a.m., Carla woke me up from one of my brief sleeps.

"They're not going away. They're getting worse," she said, grabbing my hand. She was shaking.

"OK. Then I guess it's time to go," I said. I looked deeply into her eyes, her face backlit by the hall light, and smiled, trying to reassure her.

"I'll call the doctor and let them know," she said, and I realized the shaking had stopped. Somewhere deep down inside of her, Carla had found the courage she needed to face what had started to happen. And, I realized as I got out of bed and splashed water on my face, so had I. I mouthed a "thank you" to God and got dressed quickly. The dog, thoroughly confused, rushed to my side.

Before leaving, I typed this message to our update list.

Subj: Jacob to arrive soon?

It's 2:15 a.m. and we are off to the hospital. It might be a false alarm, but the doctor wants to check Carla out. For family and friends who have asked that we call, if it's the real thing, we'll be calling. For everyone, please

124

be in deep prayer. Perhaps even fast if that is something you are able to do. I pray that God gives me the strength to be exactly what Carla needs and I pray that Carla feels God's love and strength. You'll be hearing an update one way or another...

In Christ, John

Within 40 minutes of Carla waking me up, we were in the car and pulling out of the driveway.

"We should call our parents," I said. "They said they wanted to know as soon as it was a go."

"But we don't know if it's definitely a go," Carla responded.

"Well, then this will just wake them and put them on alert."

For years I had dreamed about making the drive to the hospital with my pregnant wife beside me, breathing like a steam engine chugging down the tracks. I had dreamed of it for one simple reason: the speed. Deep down, every male has a tiny piece of Mario Andretti inside him, the part that looks for open stretches of highways to test the limits of his automobile, to see exactly why the makers of the car put numbers above 90 mph on the speedometer. My part of Mario Andretti just so happens to be a bit bigger than your average guy. From the first time my father let me ride the tractor around the yard, visions of the Indianapolis 500 filled my head any chance I got to operate a moving vehicle. Trips to go-cart tracks were like a Catholic's trip to the Vatican.

The seriousness of the situation, knowing so much was uncertain with Jacob's pending arrival, took the edge off the joy I would otherwise feel, but the inherent maleness of having the road basically to myself in the wee hours of a December weekday

Jacob's Story

morning was more than any somberness could totally overcome. So it came to pass that I pushed the limits of my Nissan Xterra, treating it like Jeff Gordon's NASCAR racer as we streamed down the highway amidst blowing snow flurries that never reached the ground. I was color blind to red lights. Speed limit signs were mere suggestions for those without a mission, and I certainly had a mission: Operation Get My Wife to the Hospital in World Record Time.

Each contraction that hit—totally random in length and spacing—made my foot heavier on the gas pedal. I was operating under the theory that even if there were a police officer shooting radar at this early hour on such a cold morning, should he choose to pull me over, he would simply serve as an escort to get me to the hospital that much quicker. Carla's composure was quickly waning as the pains grew worse. Thoughts of the breathing techniques Debbie Anderson had taught us that blessed evening in our living room had fled from my consciousness. It was while traveling at about 95 mph down Interstate 75, with a fever last gauged at 101.9 and a pain-ridden, sweating wife beside me, that God caught up to me. I was blowing it.

Slow down, I felt God say. You'll make it. I'm with you. Remember the breathing techniques. Help her. She needs you now.

My foot eased on the accelerator, though the car still sped along at a faster-than-legal clip. My mind cleared a bit and I was able to delicately tell Carla, "Breathe, honey. Remember, like Debbie taught us." I gently stroked her knee and did the "hee-hee-hee-haaaa" breathing myself to get her focused. Carla picked up the breathing with me. A smile crossed my face. The thought had struck me how funny we must look, two people flying down the highway, "hee-hee-hee-haaaa. Hee-hee-hee-haaaa"ing all the way.

When we pulled into the hospital parking lot, I was momentarily struck by a wave of panic. In all the trips we'd made to Good Samaritan, we'd neglected to figure out one thing: Where should we go if "showtime" happened in the middle of the night? I looked to the main entrance, the one we'd walked through for the dozens of appointments we'd had down here. That wouldn't work. It would most likely be locked. I scanned left. A big red signed screamed "Emergency." Well, this would classify as an emergency, I should say, at least in our lives. Carefully, with my hand around Carla's waist, we made our way to the emergency room entrance.

Three words let the emergency room nurse know what was going on: "She's in labor." With a look of understanding, she ushered us to the right place, up the elevator and to the seventh floor, where our arrival was announced with a "ding" to the nurses at the admitting desk.

Many things would shock me during the next 24 hours. The first—other than that an SUV burns up a heck of a lot of gas at high speeds—was that our situation gave pause even to the medical community. While the admit nurse asked Carla the routine questions she had probably asked a thousand times before, I broke in with, "There are complications. Our baby is not expected to live."

The questions stopped. Her fingers that had deftly been moving on the keyboard stopped. She looked up from the computer screen and directly into my eyes. I saw many versions of that same look that day, from nurses to doctors, from orderlies to anesthesiologists, from friends to relatives. The look said many things, but they all could be filed under the same heading of, "Oh my gosh, no." How many women had this admitting nurse handled in her career? How many women had come in and sat exactly where we were sitting, nervous and in some degree of early labor pain, ready to deliver healthy, vibrant babies? We were different.

Jacob's Story

The awkward moment passed and we gave the rest of the necessary information that allowed us entrance to an examining room. The contractions were coming a bit harder by now but were no less random. Carla changed into a hospital gown and tried to find a comfortable way to rest in the adjustable bed while we waited for the doctor.

Conversation was brief—at least spoken conversation. On a deeper level, though, our souls spoke to each other. I could read how frightened she was of the uncertainty of labor, let alone labor that would bring forth a child she had grown to love, a child who was safe and sound right now but who—by the very forces of her own body—would enter into a world in which he most likely was not capable of surviving. She could read how scared I was, too, scared that she was about to suffer physical and emotional pain that I had never seen her experience at any time during our relationship. She could also tell by looking at me how ill I truly was.

"How are you?" she asked.

"How am I?!?" I responded, laughing at the irony of who the questioner was. "You worry about how *you* are. I'll be OK."

Soon after, the doctor—a resident, actually—came. He was a young man, seemingly not much older than I was, and he had the bedside manner of the disinterested pet cat I had grown up with. I try to excuse this by noting how early in the morning it was or with the knowledge that residents work long, long hours, but part of me finds a doctor who comes off as uncaring worse than an unscrupulous auto mechanic. In response to his probing, short questions I gave him the rundown of what the doctors had diagnosed in Jacob and what they thought might occur. He asked further questions, using large medical words that even the past four months had not hammered into my vocabulary. All I was left able to say was "I dunno," to which he sighed and, with a pat to Carla's hand, prepared to examine her.

128

He took about five minutes and when he was done he launched into a diatribe about measurements and statuses that flew above my head. All I truly wanted to know was if she was, indeed, in labor. Finally, I interrupted him.

"We've got relatives coming from far away who want to be here. If you had to make the call, would you get them on the road now?"

"Oh yes," he said. "She's in labor."

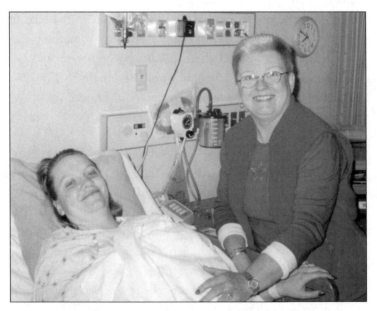

Cheryl McKee, at the hospital before sunrise on Dec. 20, 2000

Cell phone in hand, I made my way back to the parking lot for our bags. It was cold, I realized standing there, trying not to shiver as I contacted first my parents, then Carla's.

My third call was to Cheryl McKee. Prior to Jacob's diagnosis, we hardly knew Cheryl. We'd talked to her before and

Jacob's Story

after church, but the relationship was anything but friendship. After news of Jacob's condition spread around the church, Cheryl sought us out, checking up on Carla, making the extra effort to be Carla's friend and supporter. As November had rolled into December, she had made Carla promise that no matter what time she went into labor, we would call her. It was a request Carla and I wondered if Cheryl really meant, considering that the time had actually come and that time was a little after 3:30 a.m.

In the end, the decision to call Cheryl came down to who Cheryl is, an unconventional, sometimes brash, deeply honest, compassionate and loving person who marches to the beat of her own personal drummer. When Cheryl says something, she means it, and as I stood there debating whether to dial her number, I realized that 3:30 a.m. would be a perfectly fine time to call her. It was a call I am forever grateful I made.

By the time I got back inside, lugging the far-too-many bags we had packed, Carla was ready to be moved. With IV pole in hand, she walked into the birthing room and was situated. I looked around and was immediately struck by the awesomeness of the situation. This was where my son would be born. If the doctors were right, this would be where he would spend his life, in the arms of those who loved him, until he went to be with the One who loves him most. The realization of this hit me like a punch in the stomach and I quickly found the nearest chair. It had truly all come down to what was about to occur in this very room. After all the prayers, all the hope, all the worry, we'd learn what God had in store right here.

It was a nice room, not exactly spacious but certainly not small. The floors were hardwood and the walls covered with a

A Journey of Faith

few pictures meant to set harried mothers' minds at ease. The bed was centered against the far wall and took on the appearance of a toy Transformer with all the different attachments that could and would be placed on it to aid the birthing process. Good Samaritan was more of a high-volume birthing center than the suburban hospitals that had developed specialty birthing suites resembling small apartments more than hospital rooms. Oddly enough, the hospital-like feel of Good Samaritan made me feel more comfortable than if we'd been in the same situation at one of the suburban hospitals.

Carla was soon hooked up to an epidural and the contraction pain quickly subsided, leaving her with a giddy glow and statements of "These drugs are GREAT!"

Not more than an hour after I had hung up with Cheryl, she came through the open door to our room with a perky "Hello, Agliatas!" that only Cheryl could have at this early hour. Without hesitation, she went over to Carla and placed her hands on her bulging belly that created a mountain in the covers. "Jacob, are you ready to come be with us?" she said loudly. "We're ready for you."

Our first nurse entered the room just then to check on Carla. "Do you know who this is?" Cheryl asked her, pointing at Carla's belly. The nurse, perhaps a bit shocked at Cheryl's openness—as all who have known her have at some point been—looked wide-eyed and surprised. "This is Jacob. Have you said hello to Jacob?" The nurse smiled and shyly said "Hello Jacob" in the general direction of Carla's belly.

As the nurse went about setting up a variety of equipment and checking different things, Cheryl was by her side, asking "What's that?" with childlike fascination at the complex gadgets. When the nurse chuckled, Cheryl said, "Hey, we're here to learn, aren't we?"

I looked at Carla. She was smiling. That was good. If I had doubted that we should bring Cheryl in on this occasion, those

Jacob's Story

doubts faded. Cheryl immediately did something I couldn't. She set Carla totally at ease by making her laugh, by simply being the crazy Cheryl whom we had come to appreciate.

Carla was examined periodically as Cheryl busied herself with checking out every piece of equipment in the room and I sat in a chair sweating. The nurse noticed my condition and asked if I was OK. I told her about the fever, and she came back with a big glass of orange juice and two Tylenol. I started talking to the nurse and handed her a typed-up sheet I had made with our wishes.

To: the medical staff delivering our son

The time is near when our son will be coming into this world. We want to thank all of you who have had a hand in supporting us and giving us all the information we've needed to make some pretty difficult decisions.

With all the data we have received up to this date, these are our wishes for when our son is born.

If our son is born with impaired lung function, we DO NOT want him put on a respirator. We DO NOT want any heroic measures taken to resuscitate him should he stop breathing. What we DO want in the instance of his lung function being determined to be impaired is to have as much time with him by ourselves and with our friends and family members who are able to be with us as possible. There would be no need to conduct further tests on his kidneys if this is the case. If things look extremely grim, I request that he be handed to me (John) so that I might do an emergency baptism.

A Journey of Faith

If our son is born with normal lung function, we would request that everything be done as quickly as possible to determine the level of kidney function he has. We request that Dr. John Bissler at Children's Hospital (or someone in his group of pediatric nephrologists) be contacted to let him know that we want to arrange transferring our son to Children's Hospital within 24 to 48 hours where kidney dialysis can be done. Our goal is to do kidney dialysis until our son is big enough for a transplant. We know the chances of success are remote at best, but these are our wishes.

Regardless of which scenario plays out, we would request that every effort be taken to gather as many keepsakes as possible—photos, footprints, handprints, etc., anything that would help us remember our son and give us something tangible for when he is with God and we are here.

Again, thank you for your understanding in all of this. Thank you for all your hard work on this case. We have been blessed by your intelligence and your support.

I asked the nurse to share our wishes with everyone on duty so they would know what we wanted. She smiled as she read and I asked her why.

"I prayed last night that God would put me in the right place at the right time," she said. Another of God's angels.

Soon after, we heard familiar voices at the door. Our church friends, Victor and Elaine Jackson, and our church's interim pastor Larry DeLozier and his wife, Millicent, had made it. As Jacob, unbeknownst to my drug-aided and blissful wife, was starting to nudge his way into the world, the room took on the atmosphere of a family reunion, with people laughing and telling stories. Carla and I were as at ease as possible, given what we knew was coming.

Jacob's Story

Ten minutes later, we met another of God's angels, Dr. Amy Brenner.

I had never met Dr. Brenner before, though she was one of the associates in the same group as Dr. Bonar. By grace, she was the one who happened to be on call that morning and would be the one to deliver Jacob. She was friendly, young, with warm eyes, long hair and a comforting smile. She also looked nervous, something that rattled me. She was familiar with our case. Dr. Bonar had presented it and our wishes to all her associates many times during their group meetings; however, at first she seemed reluctant to play the part that God had intended for her. She even asked if we had planned on having Dr. Bonar deliver our baby. I made sure to look her in the eye when I responded, "No, we knew whoever it would be could do the job."

At 7:30 a.m., Dr. Brenner declared that Carla was fully dilated and ready to go and she would start pushing soon. I quickly went outside to use my cell phone and call my parents. My mom answered.

"Mom, it's John. Carla's flying. They said she will start pushing any time now and that the baby could be here in a few hours."

My mom lost it. I heard her cry "No!" and then the phone was handed to my father. They were stuck in traffic, still a good seven hours from Ohio. They weren't going to make it. Carla's parents weren't going to make it. And if things went as the doctors feared they might, they might not make it in time to see their grandchild alive. I hung up with sadness in my heart. I wanted to meet my son. I wanted to have all of the questions answered, but I didn't want it to happen so soon before those who wanted to meet him could get there.

I quickly went back inside and saw that our church friends were picking up their coats and hats and gloves. When they saw me come back in, Pastor Larry stopped everyone and asked if we could bow our heads in prayer. We gathered in a circle

A Journey of Faith

around Carla in the bed and held hands. I can't say I remember a word of Larry's prayer. All I remember is the power and glory in that room right then. With Carla's hand in my left and Victor's in my right, I felt God's strength pouring into my body, and for the first time since the fever hit, I had energy. When Larry said, "Amen," I knew we were ready to go.

Carla and baby Jacob, minutes after birth

Chapter Nineteen

Welcome, My Son

Carla's first hours of pushing produced absolutely nothing. Jacob hadn't budged. Dr. Brenner made the decision to sit Carla up and let gravity help out as we waited for an hour, during which we watched "The Price is Right." When it came time to push again, the results were the same at first. I would make my 10 count and Carla would push with all her might, but Jacob wasn't moving. "Maybe Jacob's waiting for his grandparents," I said, thinking at first it was a joke. Then I realized there might be some truth behind my words. Jacob had slammed on the brakes.

Carla's labor up to that point had been easy, or as easy as labor can be. She had felt some contractions on the way down to the hospital, but she'd weathered those and was soon hooked up to the epidural. Dr. Brenner's concern was that Carla wasn't

Jacob's Story

pushing right because she couldn't feel the area through which she was supposed to push. She made the decision to turn the epidural off for a while.

Almost immediately, Carla felt what natural childbirth was like. The worst of the pain shot through her back, and, though she could feel how she was supposed to push, she had trouble actually doing it because of the pain. The nurse positioned her on her side to try to give a different angle, but that didn't help much. Some progress was made, but by that time the pains were wearing Carla out and Dr. Brenner made the call to turn the epidural back on so Carla would have the strength left to do the rest of the work.

It wasn't until 1:30 p.m. that Jacob decided he was ready to come. As quickly as he had hit the brakes, he now seemed ready to join us. Carla's efforts were finally producing something. Jacob was traveling southbound. It was then that I committed my allotted one stupid-husband moment of her labor.

As Carla finished a push and I ended my 10 count, I, being a supportive husband, made the foolish mistake of saying, "That was a really good push, honey."

I don't know why I said it. I just did. And Carla wasn't going to let it pass. I wouldn't have been surprised if her head had done a complete turn while she said this, but in a voice very unlike that from my sweet, blushing bride, she said, "How the hell would you know?"

I paused. The nurse paused. The room was suddenly quiet. She had a point there. How the hell *would* I know? I really couldn't tell one push from the next. I was just counting to 10. It wasn't a difficult task, and by this time it was one I had thoroughly mastered. Having control of my duties, I guess I got a little bit cocky and tried to extend myself.

"Um," I started to respond. "I, ah, well, um." And then, by the grace of God, Carla returned to focusing on labor and left the subject of her dim-witted husband behind. I had learned

138

A Journey of Faith

my lesson, and for the rest of labor stuck to wiping sweat, counting to 10 and allowing my hand to be crushed in her vice grip.

It was after a particularly hard push by Carla that the room suddenly changed. All of a sudden, it was filled with eight nurses and doctors from the neonatal intensive care unit. One wore a headset and talked to some unknown entity back at the NICU to keep them informed of what was going on. Nurses set up the stirrups and got Carla into position for the final push.

As Carla waited for another contraction, time seemed to stop. Emotions overwhelmed me. Here were eight medical experts who, as I later found out, had been waiting for Jacob since 9:30 a.m., when it looked as if he was about to make a speedy entry into the world. They were highly trained, familiar with this sort of thing. Never in their average day did they experience the joy of a normal and healthy birth. They were all different, male and female, young and old, tall and short. But, even beyond the blue sterile gowns and paper hair covers they wore, they all had one striking similarity: the expression on their faces. It was an expression of compassion, concern and steely determination, an expression of recognition of what was about to happen and hope that they would be up to the task to do whatever they could to stop what seemed like the inevitable from occurring. In not one set of eyes was there resignation that Jacob would die.

Their expressions brought me back to reality. For the past several hours of pushing, I had gotten caught up in the rigors of doing my part to help Carla push, in focusing on the joyous miracle of birth. My heart was actually filled with a measure of happiness, godly happiness to be witness to one of His greatest miracles in the birth of a child. But the looks on the NICU

Jacob's Story

experts' faces struck me hard. The joy here would soon be met with uncertainty. Decisions would have to be made. And, if what the doctors had said for the past four months was true, tears of unimaginable sadness would fall.

"Here comes a contraction," the nurse said, looking at the sheet of paper being printed out that looked like an earthquake measurement. Just as quickly as it had stopped, time seemed to start again. From the look on Dr. Brenner's face I knew we were close.

"OK Carla, I need you to really bear down here. Ten full seconds. You can do it," Dr. Brenner said. I held Carla's hand and she squeezed it tightly. Our eyes met and I noticed a trickle of sweat meander down the right side of her forehead. She had been so brave, worked so hard. How proud I was of her!

"Let's meet our son," I said to her, barely above a whisper.

Carla starting pushing hard, her face turning bright red and her neck muscles straining.

"One, two, three, four," I began to count. When I hit "five," my voice cracked as a lump rose in my throat. Dr. Brenner looked at me and gave me a small, knowing smile. I cleared my throat and continued. When I hit "ten," Carla began to relax, but Dr. Brenner urged her to continue.

"Give me another ten, Carla. You're real close," she said.

Without hesitation, Carla began pushing again. Belatedly, I began another ten count.

When I reached ten, Carla didn't stop pushing and Dr. Brenner nodded her head to tell me this was OK. Counting went out the window and, voice cracking and tears forming in my eyes, I told Carla, "You're doing great. You're doing great. Push. Push. Push!"

There was a tremendous strain in the room as Carla pushed and Dr. Brenner reached to grasp our child while the NICU doctors readied for any possible surprise. Everything in my entire world seemed to come to a head like a rocket just before liftoff. Adrenaline coursed through me so heavily that I could feel the blood running through my veins, a feeling, I at that very moment, remembered I hadn't felt since I last stepped into the batter's box in a high school baseball game against a hard-throwing pitcher.

And then at 2:10 p.m., with a tremendous last push, Carla brought Jacob into the world.

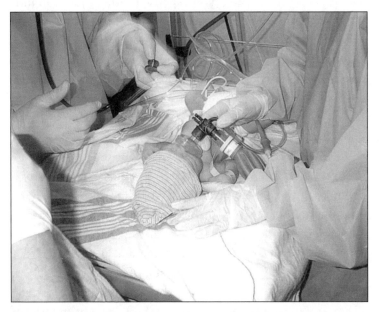

Jacob was born and immediately tended to by a team of doctors

A hundred things seemed to happen all at once. Dr. Brenner placed Jacob on Carla's chest for the briefest instant. Slimy, bloody and wrinkled, he was absolutely beautiful. Carla tenderly reached down and touched his head while I sat there, tears streaming down my cheeks. And then he was gone.

Jacob's Story

Dr. Brenner handed him to a NICU nurse who put him on the exam table on the other side of the room. That's when we heard it. Jacob cried. It was a mighty cry from a newborn who we later would find out had lungs not ready for this world. It was a cry that told us, "I'm alive. God answered your prayers. I'm alive." It was a long cry, as Jacob announced to us that he was here, that we had done the right thing by not giving up on him. It was a cry heard outside the door by Cheryl, who I later learned had long before given up sitting in the waiting room and assumed the stereotypical expectant-father's position pacing outside our door. It was a cry I believe was heard by God Himself.

Suddenly, I was conflicted and slightly panicked. They'd taken Jacob away so quickly, and my heart was instantly divided. Stay with Carla or go to Jacob. I looked deeply into Carla's eyes. God has blessed me with a wife who seems to know my thoughts even before I think them.

"Go to him," she said. "Go be with your son."

I nodded and smiled. Hesitantly, I walked over and stood behind a wall of blue-gowned doctors and nurses. Peeking over their shoulders, I saw them working on my son, hands moving quickly doing things I couldn't even tell. A tiny oxygen mask was over his mouth, a blue and pink striped hat snug on his head. There was my son. There was our child. Our child.

It is amazing to me that I went through eight months of pregnancy with Carla without fully realizing the depth of what it means to create a child. Oh sure, on some level I realized that what was growing inside of my wife was a product of us, but it wasn't until that very moment, gazing upon our child for the first time, that I realized Jacob was a creation of us—part me, part Carla. God had woven him together from the same fabric He had woven us together with more than a quarter century before.

142

A Journey of Faith

I raised my hand to my open mouth. "My God," I thought. "My God, that is my son. That is our child. That is Jacob." In doing so, my hand grazed the gown of a nurse who turned and noticed me.

"Is he OK?" I asked.

"He's breathing OK right now and he's alive," she said. "Here, touch your son." She turned her body to give me a clear path to Jacob.

"I don't want to get in the way," I said. "I want you to do everything you have to do."

"We will, but you can be with your son," she said.

She gave me an encouraging smile. Perhaps it was her eyes that told me. Perhaps it was the way her gloved hand rested on my wrist. "Go be with your son."

I moved in slowly and the doctors and nurses looked at me. A small sob escaped from deep down inside as I touched Jacob for the first time, using the back of my right index finger to gently stroke his cheek.

"It's your daddy, Jacob," I cried, totally without self-consciousness for perhaps the first time in my adult life. "It's your daddy. You just be brave, OK? We love you so much."

The doctors continued to work as I stroked his cheek, soft and warm, totally without blemish. I looked at his tiny body, his small face. He really was a combination of Carla and me, from head to toe. There was his round head, Carla's. His bigger ears, mine. His flatter nose, Carla's. His long, long fingers and toes, mine. Through the tears, I smiled.

I turned my head and noticed the door to the room was opened. Outside, I saw a bunch of familiar faces: Cheryl, Victor and Elaine, Pastor Larry and Millicent, Chuck Ullrich, a church friend, and Monica Cox, the wife of my good friend Ted. They all now stood outside the door. And then I saw two more familiar faces: Carla's parents. They had made it. They had made it.

143

Jacob's Story

I motioned for them to come in without thinking that, behind me, my wife was probably the messiest she'd been since her days as a child and was, shall we say, open to the world. I looked to her and said "Your parents. They're here. Can people come in? Is it OK?"

Smiling a huge smile through her weariness, she nodded. If she hadn't, I don't think I could have stopped the rush of Jacob's prayer warriors who streamed into the room. Carla's parents came up close to me and hugged me.

"Meet your grandson," I said as they moved to touch him. "Jacob, this is your grandma and grandpa."

My father-in-law hugged me and cried as my mother-in-law touched Jacob's cheek. Then they switched places. One by one, Jacob's prayer warriors came to meet him, to touch him, to see the reality of all that they were praying for.

I would later learn that Carla's parents had arrived in the waiting room just five minutes before. In their hurried state, a wrong turn had taken them north toward Chicago for a brief time instead of south toward Cincinnati. But Jacob had waited, and they'd made it just in time.

A voice, male and deep, brought me back to reality. "His lungs are having some trouble," the doctor said, "but with oxygen his color is good. We're going to have to watch very closely." I looked back to Carla. She nodded her understanding.

A nurse, the same one who had told me just a few minutes before to go to my son, asked me if I would like to take him to his mother. "Really?" I said. "I can hold him?"

"Yes. Go pick him up," she smiled.

Slowly, tenderly, I slid one hand behind Jacob's head and neck and the other behind his tiny body, picked him up and cradled him in my arms. "Thank you, God," I thought. "Thank you for this moment right now. Thank you so much." He was light and warmly snuggled in a blanket that matched his cap. Carefully, I made my way over to Carla's bed. The dozens of people that

A Journey of Faith

seemed to clog the room parted to give me a clear path. As I walked, I could hear the sniffles of those around me crying— friends, family and, as I later learned, nurses and doctors.

"Honey," I said when I reached Carla's bed, "here's our son." I laid him down into her waiting arms, and her tears fell fast. Her chest heaved with sobs of joy. Here he was, right there in both of our arms as we held him. Our tiny miracle.

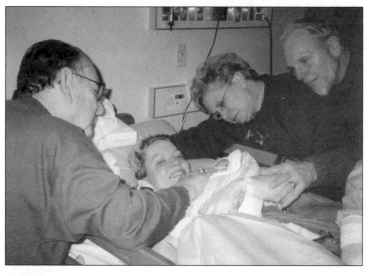

Pastor Larry DeLozier, left, baptizes Jacob while Carla's parents, Judy and Marvin Wafel, look on

Chapter Twenty

God's Child

The doctor's work on Carla done, Pastor Larry made his way over to the side of the bed with his wife, who had filled a tiny tin cup with holy water. The five of us—me, Carla, Jacob, Larry and Millicent—occupied the smallest of spaces, but there was room for God all around. As Larry dipped his fingers in the holy water and made the mark of the cross on Jacob's forehead, saying, "I baptize you in the name of the Father, Son and Holy Spirit," it was as if the room filled up with light that reached straight into my soul. All the noise from the hustle and bustle of doctors, friends and family seemed to stop. It was like God reached down and touched me, honoring me as Jacob's father, and the touch was absolutely heavenly. In the time since, I've tried to compare the feel of God's touch right then, and the best I can come up with is that it is even a thousand times better than the tiny kiss your mom gives your freshly scraped knee after putting a bandage on it when you are little.

In the silence of God's glory, with the touch of the hand of a man who four months ago had been a total stranger, our son was made a child of God, brought into the loving arms of One I believe he already knew, honored before the living God for his work, for all he had and would accomplish despite the limitations of his age and damaged earthly body.

The next ten minutes or so were loud and full of emotion. I told stories of Carla's labor and Jacob's birth as she held him in her arms. People laughed, cried, hugged and shared. All the while, I watched Jacob's chest rise and fall, rise and fall, rise and fall. It was a struggle for him, but right here, right then, we were getting what we had prayed for. We were holding our son.

Soon, it was time for the doctors to give Jacob a chest x-ray—they had brought a portable machine right to the room—and we handed him back to them. As we did, my thoughts fled to my parents. I looked at my watch. They had to be close. Where were they? I reached for my cell phone but remembered the signs on the walls prohibiting its use. I wasn't about to go outside to make the call, but I didn't have a calling card and the phone wouldn't dial long distance. Without hesitation, Monica said, "Here, use mine," and called out the numbers for her calling card. In a few seconds and after a few rings, my dad picked up his cell phone.

"Your grandson is waiting for you," I said in place of "hello."

"What? What!" he said, almost screaming. "And he's OK?"

"Right now, yes. Where are you guys?"

They were a block away from the hospital.

"Well, hurry it up," I said. "Your grandson wants to meet you."

Ten minutes later, I saw my parents in the doorway, waiting for an OK to come in.

"Jacob waited for you," was all I said and met them with a hug. When I look back and think about how things went that day, it strikes me as a godly truth that Jacob did indeed wait for his grandparents. Had things gone as they had been, as the doctors had every reason to believe they would, Jacob would have been born hours before Carla's parents arrived and even more hours before my parents could possibly have reached the hospital. God answered their prayers, however, to give them time to meet their grandson.

I took my parents over to the exam table, where the doctors' hands were once again moving faster than I really could see. I looked up at one of the doctors, who nodded his head. "You can hold him," he said.

Again, tenderly and slowly, I picked him up and handed him to my father. "Jacob, this is your grandpa."

With tears in his eyes, my father held Jacob as I picture he held me 26 years before. His eyes locked onto Jacob with such wonder and happiness, and I filled with pride. Soon after, my mom tearfully took Jacob into her arms and stroked his cheek exactly as I had done the first time I had touched him. I guess nurturing is somewhat genetic after all. She and my father went over to Carla and I watched as my mother handed Jacob to her and kissed her forehead. How blessed am I, I thought, that they get along so well.

Again, it was the doctor's voice that brought me back to reality.

"He's having some trouble breathing and it seems that there's some air between the lung and the chest cavity putting pressure on him," he said.

Jacob's Story

I looked at Carla. All the pre-planning. All that "what-if" situations we had run through, it all came down to this. It wasn't a guessing game anymore. It wasn't a fantasyland of "what would you do in this circumstance." Here was reality. Here was a real circumstance. What would we do?

For months, a fear had sometimes gripped me that when the time came to make a decision that I would freeze, that I would revert to the mental state of a little boy who looks for someone else to tell him what clothes to wear, how to comb his hair and the like. Now I knew: I would not let that happen.

"Can we please be alone for a few minutes?" I said, loud enough for everyone to hear. "Doctor, please stay. We have questions." I paused and looked around the room as people silently filed out of the room. "And Larry, can you please stay?"

I grasped his hand and he put his other on top of the link we just formed. "Of course I will," he said.

I heard the door close and it was silent. The doctor, stern and concerned. Carla and I, filled with indecision and worry. Larry, compassionate and ready. Jacob, squirming a bit and struggling to breathe. This was the reality.

We questioned the doctor on what the procedure would entail. It could be done right there, which was important to us because we didn't want to have Jacob leave our sight if possible. A needle would be inserted into Jacob's chest cavity and the doctors would attempt to remove the trapped air. The risks were that if a tear in his lung was causing the air to leak out, the needle could make the tear worse. And if it wasn't a tear, one wrong move could create one and make things worse. The procedure could also do nothing. But if it worked, it might make breathing easier. Only then would they check on the kidney function. One step at a time.

My heart ached. How much pain had Jacob endured already? Before even breathing his first breath he had been

A Journey of Faith

poked and stuck so many times. Would we be causing him more harm, needless harm, by allowing a procedure that had such a small chance of success. Was it time to stop all the medical work and just let Jacob live his life for as long as God would allow?

"Larry, could you please lead a prayer?" I asked. I took his hand in my left and the doctor's in my right. A few seconds later, the four of us had formed a prayer circle with Jacob in the middle, lying on Carla's chest.

"Lord God, you are an awesome God and we call on you right now to be with Carla and John as they face this difficult decision," Larry prayed. "Be with the doctors as they give Carla and John all the information they need to make this decision. Let this be your decision, God. We know, Lord, that you are at work in this situation. We have faith you will lead John and Carla to the right decision."

As he continued, I let God guide my mind. I simply let go of my own effort to figure out the right thing to do and let my thoughts go. "My God," my first thought was, "how I want Larry to tell me what he sees as the right answer." It was a foolish thought, I know, and I knew it then. "I don't want to do the wrong thing. I don't want to hurt Jacob, Lord."

My thoughts took me to a promise I made way back when this all started, on the road to Tennessee after the first round of procedures. As Carla slept beside me in the passenger seat and I kept the car between the lines on Interstate 75, I made a vow to Jacob—then Kix—that I would not give up on him until he breathed his last breath.

Breathed his last breath. This had everything to do about breathing. This had everything to do about my vow. A wave of certainty swept over me as I heard Larry's voice continue with the prayer—distant now. In my right hand I felt the hand of the doctor, who I now realized would be the one to insert a needle into our son to try to make it easier for him to breath.

151

Jacob's Story

"Amen," Larry finished and immediately my eyes locked with Carla's. She nodded.

"Let's do it," I said.

The door opened and people flooded back into the room. Quietly, as the doctors began the procedure, I informed everyone what they were going to do and why. People nodded, hugged us and told us we made the right decision, that they supported us no matter what we decided. And then the family reunion atmosphere picked up again. It was the strangest thing. A needle about as long as Jacob's body was being inserted into him as he lay on a table across the room while we talked and laughed and joked and hugged and shared. In my soul, there was a peace, that God's hand was right here with all of us.

Fifteen minutes later the doctor came back to us as a nurse handed Jacob back to Carla. He was somber.

"It doesn't look good," he said. "His lungs don't seem to be working properly and I don't think there's anything more we can do, short of putting him on a ventilator, which I respect that you don't want to do."

The news should have hit me with the weight of a fallen concrete wall. This man had basically just said that our slim hope was gone, the hope we'd held onto that the doctors would be wrong, that Jacob would soon die. There's no rational explanation as to why this news didn't crush Carla and me right then and there, why the tears didn't start to flow faster and the sobs come harder than ever before. But they didn't. Instead, there was a comforting peace surrounding us. We asked questions of the doctor about Jacob's kidneys—they wouldn't even bother testing them because that wasn't the problem right now—and about things we could do to

A Journey of Faith

make him more comfortable. He offered to put Jacob on oxygen that flowed through a tube just under his nose so we could hand him around more freely without the confines of the full oxygen mask.

With that, we accepted what was going to happen. Jacob, he told us, could live anywhere from a few more hours to about five or six, he estimated. And then his lungs would stop working and he would die. Silently, he left the room and we were surrounded instantly by the love of our friends and family.

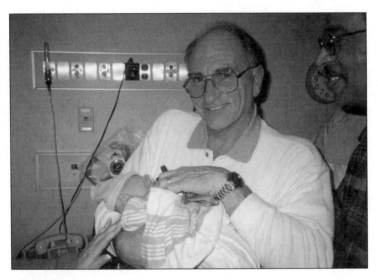

Chuck Ullrich with Jacob

"Who wants to hold him?" I said soon after. The room grew silent and people looked at me like I was half crazy. I wasn't. The reasoning was simple. While he was growing inside of Carla, Jacob had come to mean so much to so many people, especially those in that room. By blood, he was related

Jacob's Story

to me, Carla and our parents. By spirit, he was related to all of God's children—young and old—who were in the room with us that day.

Chuck smiled his sheepish smile first and said, "It would be an honor." He held out his hands and I placed Jacob in his arms. It was as if everyone else in that room suddenly ceased to exist for Chuck, as he cooed in Jacob's face and rocked him gently.

The room would get more crowded as the day went on with people who wanted to hold Jacob. Dr. Bonar, who had so tenderly guided us through that first horrific day when we found out something was wrong with Jacob, stopped by our room twice to visit with us and hold Jacob. It's perhaps the most special photo to me, with her holding our son in her arms, a tear frozen in time running down her cheek. Dr. Bonar had brought countless babies into this world, but Jacob, to her, was more than just another delivery. She had prayed for this child, she'd read the columns I'd written about him for the newspaper, and now, holding him, she knew she was a part of Jacob's family, a part of Jacob's lifetime. It moves me deeply how special this was to her.

Dr. Polzin stopped by as well, and we handed our son to him. Figuratively, Jacob had been in Dr. Polzin's hands for months, hands that carefully guided needles in and around him in an effort to find some medical way to help him. Now, carefully supporting Jacob's neck, he held Jacob up in front of his face, staring at him with wide eyes and taking in the sight of the boy who he himself had prayed for. Like Dr. Bonar, this was not just another delivery for him. This man who had shared with us our must vulnerable moments and had seen our emotions as bare as they get was also now a part of Jacob's family, a part of his lifetime.

Cameras flashed repeatedly as Jacob was handed around that day, giving us memories that we—and they—will cherish

A Journey of Faith

forever. In most of the pictures, Jacob is wrapped warmly in the blanket knitted by my grandmother—his great-grand-mother—and is barely visible. But what is so noticeable in all the pictures is the smile on the faces of the people holding him. It isn't a "say cheese!" forced smile. It is a genuine smile of happiness to be right there doing exactly what they were doing: getting to know the little boy they had prayed so often and so hard for.

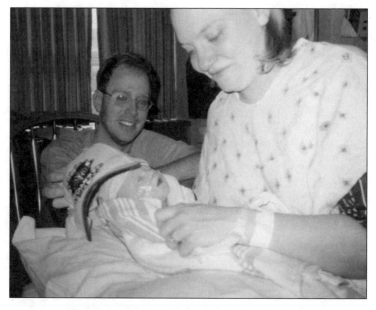

Jacob was officially made a Yankee fan just before his lungs stopped working

Chapter Twenty-One

Go Be with God

It was about 5 p.m. when fatigue hit me hard and I nearly passed out before sitting down in a chair by Carla's bed. No one noticed that I had almost missed the chair and fallen back into the wall. They were still happily cuddling and fussing over Jacob, taking his footprints, removing his diaper to get a look at his cute baby butt, taking a small snippet of his blondish-brown hair. My head swirled momentarily and my stomach itched. I shed my sweatshirt and pulled up my T-shirt to look at my skin. I was dotted with small red bumps.

Just then, my mother turned and noticed. "You broke out in hives!" she said to me. "Stress, I'm sure. That happens."

I took off the Yankee hat I had put on right before leaving the house, what seemed like forever ago, and wiped my sweaty forehead. I don't know what my fever was at that point, but it

Jacob's Story

was up there. I leaned forward and put my arms up on Carla's bed. Jacob was laying in her lap on her legs, his feet by her now-much-smaller belly.

"My boy's gotta be a Yankee fan," I said, smiling, and put my hat on his head. Someone snapped a picture as Jacob officially become another fan of the greatest baseball team in history.

It was the last picture we took of him while he was breathing.

The second I noticed his chest wasn't rising and falling, rising and falling, replays in my mind constantly. One instant I was joking about how he was part of the Yankee tradition and the next, there he was, not breathing.

"Carla," was the only thing I could say. She recognized the panic in my voice.

"No. God, no!" she said, tears overcoming her. Someone rushed past me to go get the doctor, but inside me there was no hurry. We would not allow them to do CPR, and short of that there was nothing left for them to do.

I leaned in close to him with Carla and whispered through my own tears, "Jacob, you go be with God now. You go where it isn't so hard, where you don't have to worry about lungs and kidneys. You go be with God and be brave. Thank you for being my son. Thank you for letting me be your daddy."

We all huddled close around him, and I could feel what seemed like a thousand supportive hands on my shoulders as we all cried and we all said our good-byes.

I don't know if anyone knows exactly when a soul departs the body. I imagine not, though I'm sure some have theories. I also don't know how medically rare it is for a baby's lungs to stop working but his heart to keep beating. But that's what happened with Jacob. A doctor rushed in as we cried and put a stethoscope to Jacob's chest. His lungs most certainly weren't working, but his heart hadn't given up yet.

I like to believe that Jacob's soul was still with him despite the fact that his lungs no longer were working and despite my

158

call for him to go be with God. Jacob, even when it seemed extremely improbable, had waited for his grandparents to arrive. There were still three more people steaming toward Cincinnati who wanted to meet Jacob, and, true to his nickname, Kix kept on kicking until they arrived.

It had grown dark outside and several of our friends had tearfully said their good-byes to head home when Carla's two sisters, Sara and Dyan, meekly made their way into the room with Dyan's husband, Clint, not far behind. One look at Carla, Sara and Dyan, and you can tell they are sisters. Spend any time with them and you can tell by the way they can complete each other's sentences that they are close sisters. Look at them when they are crying and you can tell beyond a shadow of a doubt they are linked by genetic and spiritual bonds.

Jacob lay peacefully and silent in Carla's arms when the three, who had left from Kansas City, Missouri, more than ten hours before, came into the room. Every five or ten minutes, Jacob's lungs reflexively would contract and he would emit a tiny gasp that tore at my soul. The doctors assured us this was in no way an indication he was suffering, that it was the body's way of shutting down. His pinkish color that was brought out while he was breathing by the oxygen tube was gone. I hugged each of our last three visitors, strengthening right then and there what was already a close bond between myself and my sisters-in-law and starting a bond that I truly cherish with my brother-in-law.

As the three hugged Jacob and we took pictures of them with him, the nurse came in quietly to check his heartbeat. It was still there, softly, fading.

"He waited for you guys," I said. "He wanted to meet you."

Chapter Twenty-Two

Together

As 6:30 p.m. rolled around, it was time for people to go. Parents and siblings said long good-byes and, just as it seemed they would exit the room, they would come back again to say something else, get another hug, touch Jacob's cool skin one more time. Then, with suddenness, we were alone. No doctors. No nurses. No friends. No family. Just me, Carla and Jacob.

I sat by Carla's bed, itching at the spots that now had migrated up to my chest and had grown bothersome behind my right ear. Jacob lay in Carla's lap, peaceful.

"You did great," I said. She smiled humbly. "You were so brave. So strong."

"You too," she said.

I laughed. "Yeah, like it's real hard counting to ten." She laughed back, a tired, weary laugh.

A Journey of Faith

She looked so beautiful despite the long hours of labor and the emotional toll the day had taken. I thought back to the day we met, a day Carla doesn't remember, in all actuality. We were both college freshman at Drake University, on a co-ed floor in the basement of a largely freshman dormitory. Carla's room was on my way out of the building and, in the spirit of friendliness, many people left their doors open. I was on my way to economics class one morning early in the semester when I passed her door. It was open and I looked in. She was pretty, a blonde-haired girl with natural good looks and a friendly smile, sitting at her computer playing Tetris—though, to this day, she swears that, though she doesn't remember the event, she was studying, not playing a computer game.

"Hi there ," I said, pausing long enough to ensure she'd say something back.

"Hi," she said, looking over from her game (or chemistry homework, depending on whom you believe). And with that, I continued on to class.

Now, almost eight years later, she looked just as beautiful, with those same natural good looks and friendly smile. It was amazing to think that on that day, eight years before, God had brought two people from different parts of the country together and started to form the bonds that would lead us to be so strong as a couple on this very day. It made me realize right then and there that we live largely oblivious to God's daily work, preferring to think of His hand present perhaps only on Sundays but certainly not as we go to the store, get our hair cut or go to economics class. With sudden awareness, I realized how so much of my life was about God either preparing me for or getting me to the point I was at in that hospital room. It's an awareness I carry with me to this day, and it helps me appreciate the fact that no matter where I am, whether on a glorious date with my wife or in a boring corporate meeting, God has orchestrated things to put me exactly in that place at exactly that time, and He did it for a reason. Because of that, my walk with God is not just a daily thing but a second-by-second thing, and it's a walk I try to model for those around me to see. It's a walk well worth taking.

"He's so beautiful," Carla said, looking down at Jacob. "We really created him."

"Yes, we did." I smiled.

A half an hour later, the nurse came in and found that Jacob's heartbeat had stopped. Officially, he was dead. She left us alone to say our final good-byes, but to me, I had already done that. What was left in our arms was not Jacob. It was almost visually evident. The spirit that God had filled him with, the spiritual breath He had breathed into him, was gone, and what was left was the broken earthly vessel that allowed us to share so brilliantly for a few short hours in God's love for children. Nonetheless, we cried as the nurse took him from our room, knowing we would never see that physical combination of the two of us ever again here on earth.

There was such an air of finality to it all. We had conceived Jacob and watched him grow inside of Carla. Through ultrasound technology we watched him move and develop. We saw and felt his taps on Carla's belly while we lounged and watched television. And then Carla ushered him into this world with a body not able to support life, a vessel broken before it had a chance. Now, as Carla lay under the sheets, there was no bulge of her stomach. The covers were flat again. And my arms were empty, so empty. They physically ached as they had after we'd moved from the apartment to our house and I'd lifted what seemed like thousands of boxes and pieces of furniture. There were no baby cries, no cooing, no fussing. The silence was painful. For four months, we'd lived for Jacob and awaited his arrival with prayerful anticipation. Right then for the first time the thought of what we'd do now that he was gone weighed on

A Journey of Faith

my mind. We'd been so singularly focused on being ready for his birth and the decisions that we faced that there suddenly was a vast void in the middle of our lives. In the silence of the room, that void seemed insurmountable. That night, I believe, it was. Our souls needed the Lord's care in a big way.

Several hours later, we were moved to a private room a few floors up on the maternity ward. As a nurse pushed Carla in a wheelchair, I walked a few paces behind, my head spinning, my eyes so dry that it seemed I was walking through a thick, marshy fog. Our room was the last at the end of the hall, massive by hospital standards and reserved specifically for parents of babies who died. Ordinarily, it would have been a lovely place, with massive windows on two sides looking out over the Cincinnati skyline, Christmas lights blinking from snow-covered roofs.

It took a little more than an hour for Carla and me to get settled and into bed. Physical and mental exhaustion were taking over quickly, but the soul-deep pain from the past 19 hours wouldn't let us sleep. Even the painkillers Carla took couldn't help her slip immediately into blissful unconsciousness. Everything felt wrong. Instead of being in the same bed, Carla shifted on scratchy sheets in an adjustable hospital bed while I lay straight as an arrow in a military style cot that in any other circumstance would have been bone crushing and muscle crippling. The absence of physical touch from Carla was wrenching.

I could see Carla's silhouette in the bed, lit by the lights from the street. It wasn't the same big-tummy shape I had grown used to in the past several months, when I had stumbled up to bed after falling asleep on the couch watching television. There was no big belly to be careful of anymore. There was just a slight bump under the sheets. Jacob was gone.

We didn't say anything for a while, but I knew she was awake and she knew I was awake.

Finally, I said: "We both didn't want it to end this way, but if it had to be this way, this was how I prayed it would be."

Jacob's Story

"I know," Carla said, and in her voice I recognized that she hadn't just been laying there; she'd been crying. "It was beautiful."

We talked about how amazing it was that so many people were there, how amazing it was that Jacob's broken body had held out long enough so all who were trying to get there could get there, how even after his lungs gave out his heart kept beating so he could meet his aunts Sara and Dyan and Uncle Clint. We both agreed: God was truly there…right there…this whole day.

"We're going to make it through this," I said. "Together."

"I know," she said, and then the tears just weren't in the background. They were right up front. I wanted to get up and comfort her, but I couldn't. Fever, lack of sleep and mental exhaustion had joined to finally sap me of my last remaining energy. I started to drift off to sleep. The last thing I remember hearing before sleep finally came was a baby crying somewhere down the hall.

Chapter Twenty-Three

God, Just Meet Me Somewhere

I awoke the next morning before the sun rose. From the rhythm of Carla's breathing, I could tell she was asleep, something for which I was grateful. She had been so strong the whole day before, so brave. I prayed silently that God gave her good rest to face what surely would be a horrendously difficult day.

I immediately realized I was hot, and I quickly discovered that my hives had not gone away. In fact, as I ran my hands over my body, there were more. I swung my feet to the floor and sat up, trying not to squeak the cot too much. On any other night, I wouldn't have slept a wink on a bed like this. I'm a light sleeper, and it seemed like the makers of the cot had purposely placed crossbars directly across every major pressure point in the human body.

Jacob's Story

Then, with sudden and intense swiftness, I realized where I was and what had happened yesterday, that it hadn't all been a dream. For months now I had woken up like this, with a silent hope that everything since August 30 had been a dream and that somehow Jacob was fine. Now I knew this dream had ended. Jacob was gone. That was the reality.

I shuffled to the bathroom, closing the door quietly before turning the light on. Looking in the mirror, I felt old. I had bags under my eyes, my skin looked pale and shriveled, and in the beard stubble under my lip I saw gray hairs. I also saw spots. Lots of spots. Spots with white heads on them. Suddenly, I realized that what I had was not hives. It was chicken pox.

Chicken pox had all but ruined my eighth-grade life. It was an early spring day when my mother first noticed the bump on my arm, a bump with a tiny white head on it. A thorough and humbling search of my body revealed exactly three more bumps with tiny white heads on them. Fear of spreading this highly communicable disease led my mother to keep me home from school for a week, a week in which we almost hourly searched for new tiny white-headed spots that never materialized. Ordinarily, it would have been cool to be home from school for a week when I felt relatively good. But this was no ordinary week. This was the week when every able-bodied eighth-grade male asked his dream girl to the Eighth Grade Dance. It was a time-honored tradition. Ask a girl before that week and you looked like a desperate loser. Ask a girl after that week and, well, the pickings were quite slim. My dream girl certainly wasn't going to be available after that week.

So there I sat for a week, playing Nintendo and generally driving my mother crazy and, sure enough, when I got back to school, not only was my dream girl going to the dance with someone else but it was with a guy who was the worst "someone else" I could possibly imagine. I went to the dance stag and it would only be by the grace of God that I would someday manage to find a wife. Such was the thinking of my eighth-grade mind.

A Journey of Faith

Now, a decade and a half later, I was finding out what a true case of chicken pox was all about. Spots covered my torso. I turned around and strained to see my back. More spots. In that tiny bathroom, I got angry. The first thought that came to mind was the book of Job. In a test that ultimately mocked the devil, God showed how a righteous man could have everything stripped from him and still, in the end, claim God as his Lord. Job had lost his family, his possessions and, finally, his health as painful sores covered his body. Here I stood, my son gone and my body breaking out in itchy, painful spots.

"God," I prayed, head bowed. "I have done everything you've asked in this situation. I didn't hesitate once when You called me to send out an update and share the amazing things You were doing in our lives. I stayed strong in You and I refused to give in to the devil's fear and doubt and worry. This is too much, though. Ease up, Lord. Just meet me halfway. Fine, not even halfway...just meet me somewhere and make something, anything easier right now."

It was a dark, dark moment. Try as I might, I couldn't stop myself from thinking that somehow I'd done something wrong to be stricken with this so soon after the worst heartbreak of my life. My prayer was a whine, the same kind that Job offered to God, to which God replied by saying, "Who are you to tell me how to do things?"

I lifted my head and looked in the mirror at my unshaved, spotted face. Then I smiled. I don't know where the smile came from, but it came. Chicken pox. Now. Dear God, I thought, You've got a sense of humor. My vision settled on a spot above my right eye, a spot that can only be described as a mega-pock, a volcanic explosion of a chicken pock. Through the chicken pox, God gave me an eternal reminder of my son. The mega pock would not heal well and I was left with what I call Jacob's Scar.

167

Jacob's Story

The morning was a blur. Carla was examined two or three times. She was starting the healing process that all women who give birth go through, and the doctors said she was doing quite well. Cell phones and the room phone rang constantly with well-meaning relatives and parents who were trying to help arrange the particulars of a funeral service. A grief counselor came and I, for the first time, realized how tough it was going to be to adjust to life as Parents of a Child Who Died at Birth. In front of us sat a fine woman, professionally trained to help parents in situations just like ours, someone who came into our room with great intentions, a kind heart and a small stuffed teddy bear with a little pearl teardrop, something she said Carla could hold when she had that feeling of empty arms. But silently, I resented this woman. Who was she to come into our lives? We didn't know her. I didn't want to know her because I knew what she represented. To me at that time, she was like the clean-up party for the Grim Reaper, sent after death had come to gauge the handiwork the man in the black cloak had brought into our lives. As she asked probing questions, I sat there smugly, guarding Carla with a fierce protectionism that was as intense as a Secret Service agent protecting the president. In my mind, no psychological bullet would be fired at my wife without going through me first, and I would be the one to stop it.

The next visitor was the doctor who had prayed with us the day before when we were contemplating what to do about Jacob's lung problem, the doctor who had been so kind yet firm in informing us of the gravity of the situation and the decisions we faced. But he, too, quickly was put on my "enemy" list when he tried to hand Carla a form authorizing Jacob's autopsy. I snatched it away from him before he could hand it to her and listened to his explanation of how Jacob's body would be trans-ferred to Children's Hospital, about ten minutes away, where a part of his kidney would be donated to the Department of Nephrology's study, just as we had requested. Children's Hospital had agreed to waive its $1,500 fee for conducting an

168

autopsy on a patient who didn't die there, something that at the time mattered little but, as medical bills mounted, became a blessing. At that time, I didn't care about fees and I didn't care about any kind actions by a doctor who would essentially dissect my son. With a scrawl, I signed the form and handed it back to the doctor, who ignored my smugness and again extended his sympathies.

One of my many prayers these days is that the people who know me only through the hours and days immediately following Jacob's death realize that I am not the mean, smug jerk they saw. I imagine in their positions as bearers of bad news and managers of tragedy that they see lots of bereaved men such as me who are so conflicted in their feelings and duties that the only way they can function is to turn everyone who could remotely be hurtful into Public Enemy No. 1. Looking back now, I appreciate the grief counselor and the doctors for all they did and all they were trying to do.

It didn't take long before I was confronted with another form of the reality that I was now a Father of a Child Who Died at Birth. I realized quickly that it was one thing to face Jacob's death while surrounded by friends and family. They provided insulation and protection from harsh questions and innocent but stabbing inquiries. It was quite another thing to step into the outside world alone.

It was an innocent enough question: "So you've got an early Christmas present, huh?" I can't even recall who asked it, other than to say it was a woman who was sharing an elevator with me as I went to bring the car around to take Carla home. At first, I didn't know what she was talking about and an awkward silence filled the descending elevator car. Then I looked down by my feet, where a clear plastic bag contained the mementos of Jacob's brief life…the hat he wore, the blanket we wrapped him in. The

Jacob's Story

obvious assumption was that we were bringing our baby home. The fact that we weren't caused such a sudden rise of anger and sadness that for yet another awkward moment I could not speak.

Carla and I had wondered in the late stages of her pregnancy what we would say if Jacob died, how we would respond to The Question: Do you have any kids? Here, less than 24 hours after Jacob's death, I was faced with one of the many forms of The Question. I could have responded, "No, our baby died" or "No, God got an early Christmas present." In the end, all that managed to come out of my mouth was a mumbled, "Yeah," and when the elevator door opened I took off for the exit, running as fast as I could with legs weakened by illness, exhaustion and lack of food.

Bursting through the door, I continued through the cold and sunny early morning breeze until I got to my car. By this time, tears had started to run down my cheeks, bitter tears, tears of disappointment. In those conversations Carla and I had had about how to answer The Question, I was adamant about never dishonoring how real Jacob was, how strong his little heart beat, how he provided so many with so much in such a short time. Now, less than 24 hours after his death, in the first opportunity to tell someone "Yes, I had a son," I had failed to be bold enough and tell of his—and His—glory. For ten minutes, I sat in my car and wept, all the emotions stored up inside me from the day before, from the four months before, pouring out.

As the final tears fell, I remembered the last time I had wept like that. The circumstances were similar. I had been sitting in the driver's seat of my car, by myself in a parking lot. And, as it turns out, those tears also were for Jacob, the child I didn't even know existed yet.

Chapter Twenty-Four

Go Out and Do Something!

It was Sunday, May 15, 2000. The embryo that would grow into the Jacob we saw seven months later was just beginning to form, though Carla and I had not a clue of his existence yet, save for the beginnings of her cheddar cheese craving that lasted through the first trimester. Looking back, the timing of everything is far too much for me to call it a coincidence. In fact, all the events surrounding Jacob's time with us have led me to not believe in coincidences at all. Rather, I believe firmly that the things going on in my life at that time—and all the time—are God's doing, and the things I previously called "coincidences" are really nothing more than the extremely evident "payoff" of choosing to live your life walking as closely as you can with Christ.

On that sunny and warm May morning, Carla and I traveled to a different church than our usual one to hear Darrell

Jacob's Story

Scott speak. Mr. Scott is the father of Rachel Joy Scott, one of the victims of the Columbine massacre. According to the friend who was eating lunch with Rachel outside of the school when the massacre began, she, already shot, was asked if she believed in Christ. When she replied "yes," her killer executed her, saying "Then go be with Him."

It was exactly a month before Mr. Scott's appearance that I had been moved by Rachel's story to write about her in my journal. I wrote:

I'm reading a book about Rachel Joy Scott, one of the 13 victims at Columbine High School almost one year ago. It has really convicted me. Here was this girl, 17 years old, who was so with You, Lord. She gave up her friends because they made fun of her when she started to walk the talk. She gave up her boyfriend when sexual temptation became an issue. She struggled mightily with her weaknesses before You. And it's just convicted me...what was I doing at 17? I didn't know You, Lord. I believed in the idea of You, but I had no knowledge of You personally. It makes me thankful that I know You now.

This has also really focused my heart on the tragedy. I can't imagine it, putting myself back in the high school part of my life. And I picture myself as a parent, watching it all unfold before me. My God. Rachel Joy asked God to do something amazing with her life in glory of Him. God listened. It just shows that prayers are answered in God's way. God answered Rachel's prayers by taking her life and using her death to glorify Him. Through Rachel's journals, the world can learn so much about the courage it takes to walk the talk. I pray for the families of the Columbine victims and I hope that Rachel Joy is up with You, Lord, and that You hold her close.

A Journey of Faith

Two days later, Rachel's story was still deeply on my mind. In my journal, I wrote.

I continue to feel so convicted by the book I read, Rachel's Tears. I continue to feel as if I fall so short of God's plan. I continue to feel like I don't even know what that plan is for me. I continue to feel despair for our nation's spiritual fall, and I pray for signs that it is still there. I want, like Rachel Joy Scott wanted, for people to see a light in me and to turn people's heads because of it. I want to be used by God for something special. If, as it was for Rachel, that means I must die, that's the way it has to be. This is God's life in me, His very breath. It's His to do as He wants.

Those words haunt me now because I realize that in my prayer I might have the answer to the question that is so hard for most people in our situation to answer: "Why?" I had written—and meant—that if my life was the price for furthering God's mission, so be it. I hadn't realized that it might be through my son's life that He would accomplish a mighty triumph.

People have asked me and I've debated whether I believe God was responsible for causing Jacob's death. The simple answer is this: I don't know; I'll ask Him when I get to heaven. On a deeper level, though, I have to say that in some ways, yes, I do believe that God was responsible for what happened to Jacob. My view comes from where I hold God in relation to humans. This view stems from the book of Job and holds that we are essentially here to serve God. As God essentially tells Job in response to his "Why me?" complaints: "Where were you when I created everything you see before you?" In other words, "Who are you to tell Me what should and shouldn't be?"

From that comes the belief that God breathes life into us for a larger purpose than simply living a human existence. Many search for the meaning of life. I don't. To me, it's simple.

Jacob's Story

If you put someone other than yourself at the center of your universe and that someone is God, then the meaning of life is to live to serve the kingdom. Anything you can do to glorify God's kingdom on earth is what you should do to fulfill your purpose in life. As it relates to Jacob, while I don't believe God actively caused his kidneys to be malformed, I believe God can take a "bad" that inevitably occurs in the randomness He allows through free choice in a fallen world and turn it into something good. The key to this happening is that the person has to be walking with God and allowing Him to work in his life. If we allow God to be the center of our lives, I've seen that He can take the bad and work it so it speaks to the meaning of life: to glorify Him.

Of course, none of this was firm in my mind when I went to see Mr. Scott speak. Carla and I had taken separate cars because she had to leave early to return to our church to serve in the nursery later that morning. Mr. Scott's speech was moving. There wasn't much new information in it for me; reading *Rachel's Tears* had inspired me to try to learn everything I could about this girl and, through the Internet, I had learned a lot. What moved me so much was something deeper, something that at the time I couldn't recognize. When I returned home, I wrote this to a friend:

> I wanted to write this now as soon as possible so I can try to get the emotions of what happened across.
>
> Carla and I went to Liberty Heights Church today because Darrell Scott was speaking, Rachel Scott's father. Rachel was one of the victims at Columbine and her dad and mother wrote the book *Rachel's Tears*.
>
> I don't know quite how to phrase this because it's so...big...but I just had a really big "religious experience" and I don't know quite what to make of it. I guess I'll start where it all starts.

A Journey of Faith

I was walking through Berean Christian Store one day after work and was on my way to the checkout counter with my Bible study that I was buying. I was definitely not looking to buy anything else, as money in our checking account was low. For some reason, a book caught my eye. It was *Rachel's Tears*, the book by Darrell Scott and his ex-wife. I bought the book and ate leftovers that night instead of going to McDonald's. I read the book in less than two days, and it made my heart so heavy, both from the evil that went down at Columbine to the way Rachel's words in her diaries convicted me of not walking the talk. It took a lot of prayer, but God made it clear to me that I shouldn't be upset about Columbine because, through the evil that won the battle there, God was winning the war and winning the next generation. Rachel always asked for God to do something great with her, and He is.

So it was quite by chance, just a snippet on Christian radio, that Carla heard that Darrell Scott was coming to the area. And when she told me, my first response was "that's really cool," but I never thought about going. Thursday driving to work, I felt like God was moving something inside me, and as soon as I got to work I called Carla and asked her to find out exactly where Darrell Scott was speaking because I wanted to go. Which leads me to today. Darrell's normal speech was condensed because it was in the context of a church service, not a special event unto itself. It was a good speech, don't get me wrong, but it was mostly stuff I'd read in the book and in related articles on the Internet, which I felt led to look up after reading the book. Darrell's son Craig was with him. He was in the library and was the one who helped lead his classmates, some wounded, out to safety. Anyway, after his talk, Darrell and Craig went out back because there was a table set up to sell the books and T-shirts and stuff to

Jacob's Story

support his ministry, and the congregation was going to take an offering to help support the ministry. Now, you know I'm not all that—what's the word—exuberant in my worship. In fact, I'm pretty much the opposite in worship and in life, always sort of trying to blend in. Well, I tell you I have never felt the Lord move my feet, but He was today. I got up in the middle of the offering and headed out to the back, to the narthex, I guess it was, where the second-service people were congregating because the first service was running late. There were a lot of people there, but I saw Darrell and Craig there and went over to them. By the time I got there, I was already starting to feel choked up, and I told Darrell that his daughter's words had convicted me and that she was a beautiful person. He shook my hand and hugged me and then I shook Craig's hand and told him that he was a very special person who God had saved for a reason. By this time, I could barely speak above a whisper I was so choked up. I told Darrell that I wanted to walk the talk like his daughter said, and he started crying and hugged me and thanked me for my words and said "now go out and do something."

I went out to my car and started to drive away. I got onto the road, but then pulled into the first parking lot I found where I started crying harder than I've ever cried in my life. All at once, I felt as if God was showing me my sins, and they are many, and it was like I was feeling the pain that those sins caused, to me, to my loved ones, to those who've come in contact with me, and to God Himself. I put my head on the steering wheel and just cried out to God, begging him to never let me forget this moment. It was weird because I couldn't tell you exactly WHY I was crying. I just was. For about ten minutes I sat there and cried and asked the Lord to never let me forget this moment, to heal me from all the hurt, to fix me so I'm walking with Him. I'm still crying now as I type this, and I don't really know why.

A Journey of Faith

I don't know if this is what people mean who say they've had a "God moment," but this is so powerful, more powerful than anything I've ever felt before, since I came to know Christ.

It's left me so confused, though. Like, What should I do now? I know it's probably too soon to know. It's only about 30 minutes after the whole parking lot thing, but what now? What does this all mean in my life? Has God been working in my life through this whole Columbine thing since the moment I stopped when *Rachel's Tears* caught my eye?

I just never want to forget how I feel right now. I never want to forget Darrell's words of "now go out and do something." I don't know what that means, but maybe it means just be kinder to people, like Rachel was. Be compassionate. Be randomly kind. I don't know yet.

So many "whys" were answered that day in May before the questions even had reason to be asked. Though I know it sounds odd and some might label it "fanatical," I believe God that day was giving me a glimpse of what was to come. It was the pure, raw emotion part of the total experience that would be Jacob. On May 15, Jacob was reality, though smaller than a thumbnail. God surely knew that this tiny human would be returning to Him sooner than we all thought. I liken it to God saying, "Here's what you're going to feel. Do you really believe the things you profess to believe in your journal? Are you really ready to be used by Me for something special like you say you are? Because if you are, it's about that time."

The tears I cried that day had no logical reason because the events that would cause them had yet to occur. But God knew. In a way, it was like the starter of a race saying "On your marks, get set..."

Chapter Twenty-Five

Home

"Go" didn't hit in many ways until we got home from the hospital. Feverish, itchy, achy and mentally drained, I walked through the door to my house to waiting hugs from my in-laws, who had stayed at our place the night before. No words were said, but tears were plentiful all around. There are some situations, I learned, where there truly are no words. This was one of them.

Around me were reminders of the life we'd left just days before. A receipt from the station where I'd filled my gas tank the day before Carla went into labor. A reminder to finish one of my staff's annual performance evaluation. A half-full water bottle on the floor by the chair I'd sat in sweating and sick, waiting for Jimmy Valvano's speech to begin.

In so many ways, it was like I was the one who had been born the day before. Everything seemed new. Everything carried

A Journey of Faith

a "first" title with it. The first time I lay in the bed since Jacob died. The first time I watched television since Jacob died. The first time I got the mail since Jacob died. What struck me hard was that, even aside from the chicken pox virus, life was now tiring. As the weeks rolled by, I realized that every day held something new for me, a situation that I'd been in perhaps a thousand times before but one that I now was encountering as a Father of a Child Who Died at Birth. There didn't seem to be anything in my daily life that was routine, and consequently, every situation was like learning how to ride a bike. There were lots of wobbles and not just a few hard falls.

Meanwhile, emotions fluctuated wildly from one moment to the next. Of course, there was sadness, deep and encompassing. The memories of the previous day were so real that I could close my eyes and still feel Jacob in my arms, still smell that newborn baby smell. But beyond that, there was physical pain. My arms, which in a perfect world should have been filled with my son, actually hurt, from my shoulders through my elbows and into my fingers. And then there was the emotion that caused me the most guilt, one that came out of nowhere and led me into the depths of some serious soul searching: Relief.

It first hit just hours after we got home. I was sitting on the floor in our bedroom, unpacking our bags from the hospital, putting Jacob's mementoes in a small pile in the corner. From downstairs I could hear the voices of my family. All at once, it hit me. It was over. For four months, there had been nothing but uncertainty. Our days were filled with doctor's appointments and test results. Our nights had been fitful periods of sleep and doubt, worry and grief. But then it hit me: There would be no more weekly appointments. There would be no more wondering. God's plan had unfolded, at least up to this point. Jacob hadn't lived. We didn't get the miracle we asked for in his healing. But now it was over. We'd run the race, and we'd crossed the finished line. I'd done everything God had asked. I'd

Jacob's Story

kept my word to Jacob that I would never give up on him until he breathed his last breath. I kept my promises. I'd done my part. Now it was over.

Two hours later, I realized this wasn't true. While I lay on the bed, sweating and itchy, I began to have that familiar nagging feeling that my place was at the computer keyboard. I rolled over onto my stomach and actually said the word, "No." I tried to sleep. I consciously slowed my breathing and waited to slip into a dream. But the nagging continued. Words started to fill my head. Sleep wasn't going to come. The race wasn't over. So I wrote to a list of e-mail addresses that had grown to 58:

Hello everyone. I hope this finds you well.

Where do I start? I guess the best place to start is by saying this: We didn't get the outcome we wanted, but Jacob's lifetime, brief as it may be, was filled with the presence of God and so much joy that we will have memories to carry with us for the rest of our lifetimes. And it ended in a way I had dreamed ever since we found out about this problem: surrounded by family and church family, wrapped in the blanket his great-grandma had made him, engulfed in the love of all of us and the love of God.

God was there in the lives of so many people. From our first nurse who the day before had prayed that she would be in the right place at the right time for the right people to our team of doctors who turned out to be strong Christians who shared in prayer with us. At around 7:30 a.m., the doctors said Carla was an hour away from starting to push. She had FLOWN through the early stages of labor. Jacob, they said, might be here within about two hours—which was great because labor is tough and all, but it stunk because my parents were still a good seven hours away, Carla's parents were a

A Journey of Faith

good six hours away and her sisters and brother-in-law were a good eight hours away, all converging on Cincinnati. But it didn't appear that they would make it to see our son. Well, Jacob took care of that. He slammed the brakes on Carla's labor and, though she pushed valiantly, Jacob kinda said, "Um, NO, I'm waiting." Carla's parents got to the hospital no more than five minutes before he was born. My parents followed an hour later. And Jacob, though his lungs had stopped working, kept his little heart beating until Carla's sisters and brother-in-law arrived to hold their nephew.

I sit here now, not really knowing what to say. Our son has gone to be with God, a perfect Father. But we miss him so very, very much. To hand him over to the doctors after we'd spent our time with him and said everything we'd wanted to say, I don't know of anything in life that will ever be harder. But through it all, there is a confidence that God is here. God was in that room with us, guiding us to make the decisions we needed to make on Jacob's life as he struggled to stay with us for as long as he could. We got to take pictures of him, a few of which are attached. We got to tell him all about those who couldn't be there with us...his loving Aunt Christy, his great-grandparents and all the people he's touched and changed in his lifetime. We got to hold him and kiss him and love him. We got to see that he had my long fingers and toes, Carla's nose and rounder head and a combination of our two chins. We got to smell that new-baby smell and tickle his little feet.

Jacob Alexander Agliata, baptized moments after birth, died in his mother's arms shortly after he came into this fallen world. There is such a void in us right now, like we are not whole anymore. I pray for God's grace in filling that void so we can be whole again. It might take

Jacob's Story

some time, but I know God will be there to comfort us and strengthen us. He already has been, even in these first 24 hours.

Jacob's funeral will be at 2 p.m. Saturday at Covenant Community Church in Fairfield. I hope all of you who can attend will do so and then come back to our place afterward for food and fellowship.

Carla is doing well recovering from bringing the little guy into the world. She was AMAZING in labor. I find it so awesome to be able to say without a shadow of a doubt: "I admire my wife." We are both grieving and have and will have our share of tears. I also have been lucky enough to come down with a WICKED case of the chicken pox, which emerged right as Jacob was coming into this world and now pretty much cover me! (So if you're coming to the funeral, I'm lookin' REALLY ugly right now! Ha.)

I don't know what's going to happen now with updates and stuff. I know this: I have never written an update that God hasn't led me to write. So I guess what I'm saying is that it's up to Him! I do know one thing: Our lives have been forever changed by your love, support and kindness. You all have been so great to us. How can we ever thank you enough? Perhaps it's a start to say that I'm glad our friendships and bonds have been strengthened. It is just one of the many, many good things to come from the brief life of Jacob Alexander Agliata.

In Christ, John

Chapter Twenty-Six

Amazing Grace

At 26 years of age, you don't expect to be planning a funeral for your child. Your parents, perhaps, but not your child. Yet there I was, on the phone with Pastor Larry, talking about what we would like to have at Jacob's memorial service. To me, it was an easy thing to say, "Larry, you were there. You saw what it was all about. I trust you. I know you will find the words." There was no particular music we wanted, no particular words we wanted said. God had been so directly involved with this situation from the start, I knew that He would work through Larry to find the right way to memorialize His little angel.

As the day approached, the worst of the chicken pox virus took hold. The spots multiplied, the itching was unbearable and the flulike symptoms knocked me out. I'll never know how much of the lethargy and reclusiveness I felt during those first

Jacob's Story

few days after Jacob died had to do with my son's death and how much of it had to do with chicken pox. In the end, I guess it's not important, but I still wonder.

By the time Saturday morning came, I was at my absolute worst, tired and weary from the grief, unable to sleep because of the itching, still running a fever and facing the prospect of burying my son. I wasn't a fun person to be around. That all changed midmorning while I was putting my suit on, trying desperately not to rub any of the pox and start an itching frenzy. The doorbell rang and I heard familiar voices downstairs.

My Aunt Pauline, who also is my godmother, had arrived from New York. She'd been driven by her youngest son, my cousin Tommy. They'd started in the middle of the night, traversing the hilly terrain of Pennsylvania before first light and making their way into Ohio just as the sun rose. They would be turning around that night and doing the same drive in reverse so Tommy could be at work Monday morning. It was enough to move me to tears. You learn a lot about people during times of grief. I already knew my aunt was a kind-hearted and loving person who was not shy with her affection to her godson. But Tommy—a great practical joker about ten years my senior who once accidentally smashed me above the left eye with a pool cue when I drove my little tike bike too close to where the big people were playing Eight Ball—that was a different story. Tommy is a man's man, a guy who knows all about the inner workings of a car, a guy who rides dirt bikes as a hobby. Yet here he was, in my living room, asking me for a picture of Jacob that he could keep, talking to me about how sorry he was that Jacob had died. It meant more to me than anyone else who was there that Tommy had expended so much effort to come and was so transparent with his emotions. I learned that day what kind of person Tommy really was.

We got to the church early. A few familiar faces greeted us, church friends who would be singing or playing the piano in the service. My eyes immediately went to the front of the sanctuary, where Jacob's body rested in a closed coffin. It was so tiny. To think that there ever had to be a coffin made so tiny broke my heart. To realize that the broken earthly body of my son was inside was even worse. The voices around me seemed to disappear, and if anyone had been talking to me I surely did not hear. I opened the doors, walked into the sanctuary and, with Carla by my side, made my way up to the coffin.

I didn't know what to feel. I just knew I needed to be near him. I knew his spirit wasn't there. I'd seen the difference in him between when he was alive in my arms to when he had died right before the nurse took him away. But there was just something that seemed so fundamentally wrong about him being at the front of that sanctuary alone.

When I reached his coffin, I didn't say anything. I just stood there with Carla beside me. From behind me, I felt my father put his hand on my shoulder. We cried. And then we sat down in the front row. Time passed and I could hear more voices behind me, but I didn't turn around. Part of it was because of the chicken pox and how grotesque I looked. But a bigger part of it was that I just didn't know what to expect and what I'd see. Ever since we found out that Jacob might die, I had from time to time, wondered what his funeral would be like. Who would come? How many people would there be? Now, just two days before Christmas, my thought was that there wouldn't be too many for a baby who lived just five hours and died at a time when most flights were booked and many roadways were covered with snow.

As soon as the service began, I knew God had indeed worked through Larry to come up with the right way to memorialize Jacob. By using the e-mail updates I had sent, he weaved a picture of what it meant to honor God even when we don't understand him, what it meant to be a child of God and what a special child of God Jacob had been. He talked about what a lifetime was and said that Jacob had accomplished more in his

Jacob's Story

brief five hours than many would accomplish in a century. And then he turned it over to Elaine Jackson, who had just three days before held Jacob in her arms and been there when he died. Blessed with a beautiful voice, she asked people to open their hymnals to "Amazing Grace," and then she began to sing.

At first, it felt like my heart stopped. From behind me came such a beautiful sound that my eyes, which had been dry during the service up until this point, immediately began to tear. For the first time, I turned around. That's when the tears really came. The church was packed. Two days before Christmas, for a child who lived just five hours, more than 70 people filled the room. Friends, family and co-workers. Unfamiliar faces that would introduce themselves at the end of the service as some of the strangers who had supported us via e-mail after reading my columns in *The Oxford Press*. From the corner of my eye I saw the big, warm brown eyes and spikey hair of Dr. Bonar, our first angel. Tears streamed down her cheeks. On the other side of the room was my boss, retiring at the end of the year after almost a half-century in the newspaper business. Near him was my cousin Tommy, shedding tears along with me. A few rows behind them was Debbie Anderson, our childbirth class angel. They all were singing about God's glory and how amazing His grace truly is. I turned back around and for the first time since sitting in the car in the hospital parking lot just before coming home, I sobbed. God's grace had amazed me. It had filled His house with so many kind-hearted people who came to share not just in Jacob's death, but also in his life.

Chapter Twenty-Seven

Jacob's Legacy

In the time that has passed since Jacob was born and died, there's not a day that goes by that I don't think about him, sometimes with tears of sadness, sometimes with a smile that only a proud father can know. I wrote one last e-mail update at God's urging, a Christmas morning message that I typed before the sun rose on the birthday of our Savior.

> Hello everyone. Merry Christmas to you. I felt led when I woke up this Christmas morning to write to all of you.
>
> About 70 people were able to make it on Saturday to little Jacob's funeral services. Seventy people for a boy who lived only five hours...so very, very touching to us. It was kind of amazing to me because we were one of the

Jacob's Story

first into the church and sat in the front. I had no idea how many people were in the church until we started to sing "Amazing Grace." When I heard how many voices there were, I really lost it. It meant so much and was a testament to how much God had worked through this situation.

The kindness of others has been truly astounding to us. From cards to letters to little gifts to help us keep Jacob close to us, we've been so blessed. Little teddy bears, anonymous poems in the funeral guest book (please, please, please e-mail me if it was you who left it there because it was beautiful), flowers and visits from long-unseen relatives. God is good and His people are good.

Carla and I lay in bed that night before falling into exhausted sleep. We talked about how burying our little boy was hopefully the hardest thing we will ever have to do but how, when we look back on the day, we will remember it more with a smile than with tears. A smile that recollects the beauty of his funeral service, the wonderful time of fellowship at our house afterwards and the realization that God gave Jacob a voice to reach so many people. I don't think we'll be comprehending the true effects of that last one for a LONG time.

Carla is doing well. Healing well and moving around better. She's been so strong. My chicken pox, after a few MISERABLE days, is healing, though my face will frighten children (and most adults) until the scabs disappear.

We have many, many times of tears, where the realization that Jacob has died is so quick and strong and painful that one minute you're watching a football game and the next minute it's like you've been punched in the stomach. Soon, all the family will have gone back to

A Journey of Faith

their homes and it will get much quieter up here and that will be hard, but it is something we have to face. (We will certainly face it with full bellies, thanks to you guys!!!!)

God has been so comforting in these days. He has given us times of peace. He has given us His tender gift of sleep to rejuvenate us. He has given us His shoulder during the tough times. I've said this before, but how I pray that each and every one of you can at some point in your lives feel how REAL God is. It's so difficult to explain what I mean by that, but my prayer is that you will all feel what I mean. When you do, let me know.

Thank you to all who could not be here but called. Carla and I both agree: That takes tremendous courage because it's so hard to know what to say. As many of you have said, "I don't know what to say," but in calling, you're saying more than you'll ever know.

To all of those who have been able to stop by and who THOUGHT they had had chicken pox but who start itching in about two weeks…we're moving to a place without a phone. And no doors. Outside America. It's a bad neighborhood so you probably wouldn't want to come anyway. :)

Have a Merry Christmas everyone, and if I don't get to write to you before then, a Happy New Year. The year 2000 was miraculous in so many ways. Yes, it was truly tough, but it was wonderful just the same. I pray 2001 is wonderful for all of you.

In Christ, John

The time since Jacob's death has been a roller coaster. During the first six weeks, I did remarkably well. I felt loved,

Jacob's Story

supported and cradled in God's arms. And then, things changed. Phone calls stopped. The mail got lighter and lighter. My e-mail box was filled more with junk mail than the messages of support and encouragement and love we'd been getting since the end of August. All of a sudden it was, in a word, quiet.

Every time Carla ran into someone who knew what had happened, she would be met with a hug and a "How are you doing?" Her friends would call her to check up on her. E-mails still came her way. But for me, there was nothing. People would ask Carla how I was doing, but they never would ask *me* how I was doing, if I was OK. I began to feel like a person everyone talks about, but no one talks *to*. And I got bitter. I stopped going to church because I felt like I was being stared at instead of talked to. I wouldn't answer the phone when I was home alone because I couldn't handle one more person saying, "How's Carla?" without recognizing that Jacob's daddy was broken into a million pieces inside.

And then I got bitter with God.

"Where are You, God?" I screamed. "How could You leave me now?"

For a month I carried around a chip on my shoulder along with a lone-wolf attitude. All the things that people wrote before Jacob was born, they didn't mean anything because, now that Jacob was gone, where were they? My life spiraled into a simple existence of work and home life. It took a figurative smack in the face to wake me up to God's truth.

It was a Sunday evening on another day in which I didn't go to church. Carla and I were sitting on the couch when the phone rang. Pastor Larry had had a heart attack. We made it to the hospital just before he was helicoptered away to a downtown hospital that had a more specialized cardio-care center: Good Samaritan Hospital, the same place Jacob lived his life.

It didn't hit me until we pulled into the parking lot of Good Samaritan, the same lot we'd parked in during the early

A Journey of Faith

morning hours before Jacob's arrival, how difficult this was. We'd have to go through those same doors, walk down that same long hall, take the same elevator we had the last time we were here. Carla and I both paused and looked at each other. And then we just simply did it. We got out of the car, we went through those doors, we walked down that hall and we got in that elevator. Our pastor, our friend, our Uncle Larry, as he had come to be known in the time since Jacob's death, was in need.

As we approached the waiting room, we heard familiar voices around the corner. When we entered the small area, there were the faces that matched the voices. Our friends. Those who had come to experience Jacob's life had come to support our pastor and friend. We hugged. It was like a reunion. I don't think it was lost on anyone that we were all together again in the same place, united in prayer for another. The roles had changed slightly. Instead of leading the prayer, Larry was in a hospital bed fighting a fight he would ultimately win. Instead of being the one receiving prayers, I now joined in offering them for a man who had grown to mean so much to us, the man who had symbolically ushered my child into God's fold by baptizing him.

I realized right then that God hadn't gone anywhere during my month of bitterness. Though people had not come right out and asked how I was doing, they were praying, I would learn. They cared. But I had withdrawn. And in the absence of obvious support among my fellowman, I had blamed God. In doing so, I'd crawled out of God's loving hand. But that night I realized that, despite my bitterness, despite the fact that I'd blamed Him for problems of my own creation, God's hand was right there for me to crawl back into. So I made a choice that night. I crawled back into God's hand and accepted His loving comfort.

That doesn't mean that there still aren't tough days. The worst thing is that I can feel them coming several days before they actually hit and have, as of yet, been unable to find anything to stop them from coming. But in facing these tough

Jacob's Story

times, I have grown in the Lord and realized many things about the human condition, God and His dealings with us during this lifetime.

I've learned that there's much to be said about living life in the valley for a while. Before Jacob died, I would have said that the peak was the place to be. That's how I'd lived most of my life, striving to get to the top, whether it was in recreation, sports, relationships or work. Being on the peak is exciting. The view is great. The air is refreshing. The peak is small. There's not a lot of room for others, so if you're there, you know you're someplace special, someplace others are not. To get to that peak, you have to climb and, once you're there, you can look back at where you've come from easily and with pride, saying, "I've accomplished something." In that sense, the peak gives you perspective. But when your son dies or, for that matter, when you face any life-jolting grief, you realize a lot about peaks. For one, you realize that being on a peak is a fragile and dangerous balance. And because the peak is so small, you realize there are not a lot of other people around to help you hang on. You realize that when you're on the peak, you are exposed to the elements. If the wind whips up, it's going to hit you hard. If the temperature plummets, you're going to get cold fast. If the sun comes out, you're going to get burned.

Before Jacob died, I would have told you that the valley was the last place I wanted to be. Because of the peaks on either side, you get less sunlight in your life. It's cool. The air is turbulent, buffeted by the winds bouncing between the peaks. It's not really a challenge to be in the valley. You're simply there in this vast land that just about anyone can get to. There's not that special feeling about it. And if you look to your left or your right, you realize that if you want to see something new, you've got a long way to climb. But after Jacob died, I realized something about valleys. It was counter to what my first instinct was when I landed after Jacob's death. By God, that instinct told me, get climbing and get back to the top. The problem was, the

A Journey of Faith

mountain was covered with ice. No matter how hard I tried, every time I got somewhere up the mountainside, I'd take one bad step and come sliding back down into the valley with nothing to show for my climb but bumps and bruises from the rapid descent. It took numerous—too many—attempts at climbing before I stopped and looked around the valley where I lay.

It was quiet down here. It was shady. It was comfortable. It was lush with life. There were lots of people around, people who helped me get back up, helped dust me off and helped treat the wounds from the fall. What, then, was the rush to climb? Why continually drag myself up that mountainside when God was doing everything but directly telling me to stay where I was and bask in the healing comfort that the valley offers? There would be a time when the mountainside wouldn't be so slippery, a time when the ascent would be safer. Then, I would climb. And I'd climb with the knowledge that should—or should I say *when*—I fall again, I'll know more clearly from where I came.

I also learned a lot about suffering. There are some in the church community who would believe that if you aren't smiling and proclaiming God's joy, you can't possibly be a good Christian. After all, aren't you filled with the Holy Spirit? But God's love runs much deeper than blind joy. As a society, we're trained to avoid suffering at any level. Whether it's the explosion of medical advertising pushing pills, creams and other fix-me-now remedies or the prevalence of pop psychology that teaches us to pin our pain on anyone except ourselves, there is little out there touting the *benefits* of suffering. Yes, the benefits of suffering.

Suffering is different from wallowing. When we wallow, we take pain and turn its effects inward so that all we are focused on is the pain itself. But when we suffer, we are faced with the opportunity to take the pain and grapple honestly with the emotions that come from the bad things that can and do happen in our lives. Suffering doesn't have to be an end. It

Jacob's Story

can be a means to bettering our lives. When we can look at the bad things that happen in our lives and, instead of blaming God or Satan or our parents, seek to become a better person when all is said and done, we are reaping the benefits from suffering. That's why suffering shouldn't be avoided. The bottom line is that suffering is put in front of God's children to teach us something. If you follow the "happy Christian" model, you'll miss not only the opportunity to learn something, but also the chance to better yourself and those around you.

Which all leads to what I think it's really all about. Are you happy? That question seems to be at the forefront of so many people's lives. Being in a state of happiness serves as a goal, something that we strive for in our daily lives by looking for ways in which we can maximize the desired outcome. I used to think that being happy was a goal. We're conditioned to think that way. From the time we're born, we're judged on our happiness: "He's such a happy baby." As toddlers we seek happiness in a selfish way that only a child could get away with, often by taking toys right from the hands of others because doing so produces the desired state of being.

Things don't change much when we become young adults. We are told to find a job we like because being happy in a field you'll be in for the majority of your life is key. And once we get to that majority of our life, we live for those times when happiness is the king, when we get that promotion, when we buy that expensive car, when we take that dream trip. So are you happy? I answer that question with another question: Does it matter?

I'm not saying that happiness is a bad thing. If I had my choice, I'd take happy over almost any other state of being. What I am saying is that it should not be the *goal* of life. To me, happiness is a byproduct—a side effect, if you will—of something much larger, a goal much more focused on the reality of how life actually plays out. As I went through life following Jacob's death and God turned my heart to be acutely more

A Journey of Faith

aware of the pain others around me were experiencing, I was left with one question: Is this life mostly one big stormy sea with a few calm spots or is it peaceful sailing with a few spotty storms? Looking at the big picture, I was forced to say it is the former. We seem to career in this life through a sea of stormy weather, trying to maintain control as our ships are scarred and we lose precious cargo. The calm spots are few and far between. Thus, I concluded that if people in this lifetime are seeking happiness as their ultimate goal, we're going to be a society of failures. The pursuit of happiness, one of the bedrocks of our independence, is a hapless venture. The harder you seek it, the more elusive it becomes.

So what, then, is the goal if it is not happiness? The goal is to weather this life's storms in a manner that gives glory to the God we seek to serve. I know without a doubt that that's where it's at and that, lo and behold, an unintended consequence of living this way is that I'm happy. More important, though, is that living a life with this goal constantly puts me in places to help others.

The bottom line is this: Bad things happen all the time. Cars collide. Cancer strikes. People kill. Parents pass away. Babies die. In the midst of the depths of this despair is a lesson: Keep breathing. You'll never always be happy. But if you adjust your sights and change your goal, you will always have a chance to make a difference in the lives of others. Jacob did in just five hours of time with us. Remember, grief will come. But in the depths of your deepest grief and sharpest pain comes the greatest opportunities.

We miss Jacob. We go about missing him in different ways. I visit his gravesite frequently and sit in front of his gravestone or on the nearby bench in front of the huge cross where I stood on that nippy fall day with my father when we picked Jacob's final resting spot. Carla rarely goes but rather spends more time talking about Jacob with friends and family, more time in his nursery. Together, we talk about him often, sometimes with laughs, sometimes with tears. Early on we came to

Jacob's Story

the realization that nothing will ever replace Jacob. Having another child won't. Time won't. There will never be a time when we don't miss the fact that we won't have the opportunity to parent Jacob.

But the bottom line in our lives is that life has to go on. We can never be solely defined as Parents Whose Child Died at Birth. There has to be something more. Jacob's life meant something. It stood for something, in our lives and in the lives of many, many others. In the guest book at Jacob's funeral, someone slipped a sheet of paper with a poem on it, written in pencil. We have never found out who wrote it, but it speaks to the impact Jacob had in others' lives. It read:

Thank you, John and Carla, for letting us in
The hopes and dreams for a child of God
to be ours to love and hold close
Thank you for sharing your faith and hope
for a miracle, for that's what is needed.
We are a family and as such we prayed and believed
and cried with you. We all grew in our knowledge of
blest ties and binding together. Even now pain and shock
are ours. No one is ever ready to say good-bye.

Thank you sweet Jacob, what an angel came here
and helped us look to heaven right here.
You held us together in faith and prayer.
Love was ours, with more to spare
You've got a lot of family here
who are shedding a lot of painful tears.
But He who sent you to us has you now
under his strong wings and is smiling.
Baby Jacob, well done. We'll hold you for eternity.

For five hours, God gave Jacob to us to hold and love and cherish. And then He called him home. We take comfort in the

196

A Journey of Faith

fact that there is a lasting legacy that came from our son. God used him and he used us to further His kingdom. Whether Jacob brought anyone to Christ, deepened some people's relationship with God or just made a parent hold onto their child for that second longer before sending him off to school, he moved people and changed people. In short, he lived a life that God wants all of us to live.

Well done, my son.

Acknowledgments

God's path is not promised to be the easiest path. But if we ask for company when we face those hard times, God is quick to respond. Some people say this is the old "misery loves company" thing. I say it's seeing a little glimpse of heaven right here on earth. I'm grateful beyond words to those who contributed to helping make this book become a reality. Writing about the brief life of my son has been exhilarating and exhausting, glorious and gut-wrenching. If not for the encouragement of God's angels here on earth, it is a project that would never have been completed.

Carla, my beautiful wife, has been my inspiration. When it came time to write a particularly hard part of this endeavor, all I thought of was the way she tenderly held our boy in her arms. That got me moving again. Without her love, understanding and gentle hand, this never would have been completed. She pushed me to write when I wanted to avoid the pain, reminding me that part of God's plan is to help others through what we have experienced. She comforted me when the emotions got to be too much and gently encouraged me to continue. I am forever grateful to have such a wonderful life partner.

Pastor Larry DeLozier has been a constant source of encouragement, unafraid of getting in the trenches with me in my grief and showing me that there was indeed a story to tell. I am grateful for his wisdom, love and faith in me.

Jacob's Story

My sister, Christy, has been my rock, an always-available ear to listen to the tough times, no matter what the hour or situation. Her persistence and love has helped give me the words that fill these pages.

My family's love and support has meant the world in rebuilding my life. I am grateful for the cross-country treks taken to be with Jacob during his brief life by my parents, Jack and Nadine Agliata; Carla's parents, Judy and Marvin Wafel; Carla's sisters Sara and Dyan; and Dyan's husband and my brother-in-law, Clint Miller. Being a part of two families—one through blood and one through marriage—that exhibit love so wonderful is truly a blessing.

Sandra Aldrich, an author of immense talent and person of even greater character, has also been a voice of inspiration in introducing me to the book-publishing world. Her encouragement has led me through the periods of doubt that this was a book not worth writing. I am grateful to have met her as a boy through her daughter, Holly.

Lastly, though this book is called "Jacob's Story," it really is a story of the hundreds and then thousands of people who took up the cause of a helpless little one and lifted him to the Lord in prayer. It's the story of what God's people are like when they unite in heart and prayer. It is all of those people who have given me a story to tell. Thank you to those who shared in Jacob's life in such an intimate way, from the strangers who sent e-mails and cards of support to friends who went out of their way to be a part of Jacob's brief time with us: Cheryl McKee, Larry and Millicent DeLozier, Victor and Elaine Jackson, Chuck Ullrich, Monica Cox, Dr. Kim Bonar and Dr. William Polzin.

And, as Elaine likes to say to wind up our time of worship on Sunday, all of God's people said…Amen.

John M. Agliata
November 2, 2001

About the Author

John Agliata is the publisher of *The Oxford Press*, a community weekly newspaper in Oxford, Ohio, and a member of Covenant Community Church in Fairfield, Ohio. He grew up in Pound Ridge, New York, and graduated from Fox Lane High School before attending college at Drake University in Des Moines, Iowa, where he graduated in 1996 with a degree in news editorial journalism.

Jacob's Story
Order Form

Postal orders: 943 Greenwood Court
Trenton OH, 45067

E-mail orders: JacobsStory@aol.com

Please send *Jacob's Story* to:

Name: _____

Address: _____

City: _____ State: _____

Zip: _____

Telephone: (_____) _____ E-mail: _____

Book Price: $13.00

All proceeds from the sale of this book will be donated to children's charities.

Shipping: $3.00 for the first book and $1.00 for each additional book to cover shipping and handling within US, Canada, and Mexico. International orders add $6.00 for the first book and $2.00 for each additional book.

Or order from:
ACW Press
5501 N. 7th. Ave. #502
Phoenix, AZ 85013

(800) 931-BOOK

or contact your local bookstore